COLEFAX & FOWLER
THE BEST IN ENGLISH INTERIOR DECORATION

Chintz in glorious faded colours, curtains meticulously swagged, fringed and tasselled, the most comfortable upholstery and expertly applied paint finishes, all set in timeless interiors and discreetly lit to show off beautiful antiques and paintings. These are the hallmarks of the style developed by Colefax & Fowler in the post-war years and currently more fashionable than ever.

This informative and fascinatingly anecdotal book tells the story of the firm's founder, John Fowler, and shows his style evolving through his association with Sibyl Colefax and Nancy Lancaster and later through his work restoring National Trust houses. It describes the expert craftsmanship and technical skills which produce the ageless Colefax & Fowler look and shows examples of their current work in different types of room in a wide variety of locations, ranging from Badminton and Sudeley Castle, large and small country houses, to flats and mews houses in London and abroad.

COLEFAX & FOWLER

THE BEST IN ENGLISH
INTERIOR DECORATION

CHESTER JONES

PLANNING AND RESEARCH BY ELIZABETH DICKSON

A Bulfinch Press Book
Little, Brown and Company
Boston   New York   London

FIRST UNITED STATES EDITION, 1989
FOURTH PRINTING, 2000 FIRST PAPERBACK PRINTING, 2000
FIRST PUBLISHED IN GREAT BRITAIN BY BARRIE & JENKINS LTD.

ISBN 0-8212-2452-5 (PB) 0-8212-1746-1 (HC)

LIBRARY OF CONGRESS CATALOG CARD NUMBER 89-61686

BULFINCH PRESS IS AN IMPRINT AND TRADEMARK OF
LITTLE, BROWN AND COMPANY (INC.)

PRINTED IN ITALY

Contents

PART I

THE EARLY YEARS OF
COLEFAX & FOWLER

JOHN FOWLER TOOK THE ROMANTIC SPIRIT OF LATE EIGHTEENTH-CENTURY decoration, the simplicity of rural life with its celebration of nature, and fashioned it into a style of his own. The freshness and originality of his work was such that he became the seminal influence on English decoration in this second half of the twentieth century.

Colefax & Fowler today still abides by the basic principles that evolved from his working life, first as a decorator on his own then briefly with Lady Colefax and, finally, in his often stormy partnership with Nancy Lancaster. Although she only participated on her own homes, the influence of her extraordinary ability was a key factor in John Fowler's development as a decorator. Consequently Colefax & Fowler's heritage is the embodiment of the best of their work together, a blending of style, colour and pattern, lightly handled and painterly in approach. Floral chintzes are balanced by plain cottons, silks and the occasional stamped velvet. Table lamps with shades of pleated silk and card diffuse the light; English furniture, four-square and sensible, is relieved by the delicacy of a French piece. Whether painted or veneered, the furniture is kept mostly light in tone. Often an ugly colour is introduced, such as a faded black or drab, to give counterpoint to colours that are sweet and clean. The occasional highlight of distressed giltwood and the warm patina of ancient paint are all part of the grammar. The mood is then personalized by the addition of prettily painted creamware, *tôle*, pictures and prints; the fragrance and colour of flowers complete the decoration.

Fowler embraced the challenge of the most noble rooms as wholeheartedly as he delighted in the modest charm of the rustic. He loved architecture, but pressed everything he encountered into serving the fruits of his imagination. His rooms are a celebration of life and are therefore about people, and about comfort, in its fullest sense. This book traces this tradition from its origins and follows its influences through to the many examples of our work today.

CHAPTER 1   John Fowler – The Formative Years

JOHN FOWLER IN 1945 WEARING a Prince of Wales check jacket against a background of *toile de Jouy*. His appearance – smart and assured – belies the difficulties of having to work under the severe restrictions of post-war shortages.

OPPOSITE: THE DRAWING ROOM at Hay's Mews, Mayfair, designed by John Fowler, was one of his favourite rooms. What had once been a pair of mews houses, built by William Kent to serve one of the great houses in Berkeley Square, was knocked together and the first floor bedroom was used to create a grand double-height reception room. This job was completed in the early 1950s when Fowler first began to realize the importance of architecture.

THE RECENT GROWTH OF INTEREST IN TRADITIONAL DESIGN AND historicism can be seen everywhere. Each year greater numbers of visitors tour Chatsworth, Blenheim and other fine country houses and more protestors fight to save any threatened Georgian terrace or Classical building of even the most modest importance. People seeking to recreate the harmony of our more elegant past in their own homes have a wealth of specialist shops to serve them. The thirst for antiques and for all the tokens of our cultural heritage appears to have cast the eighteenth century in particular in the light of a golden age. The tranquillity promised by having such things around us satisfies a deep need that is denied by most present-day alternatives. It seems that the past inspires our enthusiasm because it represents values of greater permanence than the mere ephemera of fashion or the tyranny of design obsolescence.

In our time, the most accomplished interpreter of these traditional aesthetics was John Fowler. His influence as a decorator has been immense, much wider than the knowledge of his work. He started from modest beginnings in the early 1930s, reaching maturity in his work just after the war. It was therefore the period of the 1950s and 1960s, followed by a few extra years during which he continued to work for the National Trust, after his retirement from Colefax & Fowler in 1969, in which his most glorious contribution was made. His early years are interesting because he was almost entirely self-taught. He was artistic, and had a passion to learn; with the skills he acquired in the craft jobs he undertook in his youth, he finally emerged as the principal decorator of his time. The authority of his work complemented the many fine buildings on which he was privileged to be engaged. From his feeling for architecture, and with his inspired handling of colour and furnishings, he created interiors that are truly memorable. Schelling, the eighteenth-century romantic poet, observed that architecture is 'frozen music'; in John Fowler's hands an interior became a perfect minuet.

He was fascinated by history, and for him it lived in a way that few people appreciate. His interest was not limited to the great events of the centre stage; it was the minutiae of life that absorbed him, the details that historians pass by. His knowledge of, and enthusiasm for, the life that went on within the great country houses, are constantly referred to by his clients. For him, it was a romantic story that was constantly extended through fresh discoveries and realizations. He took great trouble to find out how houses had been organized in the past, what people ate and wore, about their amusements and their music, both above and below stairs. The picture in his mind was a complete one, so that when it came to decorating a house he understood the exact historical context to which it belonged. Sometimes his enthusiasm for detail carried him away. In one instance, two women, who had come to him for advice in the early days at 292 King's Road, stamped out after an hour's lecture on the domestic life at Uppark in Sussex. 'We did not come here to listen to all that; all we wanted were some curtains!' they exclaimed with obvious irritation.

Most of his clients, however, were caught up in these enthusiasms

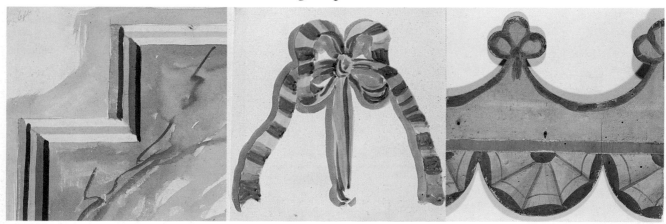

and benefited from the knowledge of the finer historical points that lay behind his recommendations. To him, furniture, pictures and objects were history brought to life; even the most modest item would speak to him with as clear a voice as an artifact of major importance. In fact, the humble had special significance for him and throughout his life he would choose this minor key in which to live himself. 'Humble elegance' was what he called it, and in his hands the effect was charming and delightful. It was a preference that perhaps was rooted in the humility of his background.

His childhood and youth threatened an unpromising future. He left Felsted, his school, in 1923, just before his seventeenth birthday; his father had deserted his family and died when John was only nine. He later confided to a friend that he had loathed his father and had been bullied at school, and he never talked of his elder brother Richard. He adored his mother, who is believed to have had considerable taste, which she fortunately passed on to her son. Although she could never afford any sort of professional training for him, she nonetheless encouraged him in artistic pursuits.

In his teens his interest in art and all visual things prompted him to bicycle around, looking at antique shops, villages and churches. Thaxted Church, in Essex, made a particular impression. This church, under the auspices of the socialist Rev Conrad Noel, embodied the spirit of the Arts and Crafts Movement. Mrs Berry, otherwise the decorator Margaret Kunzer for whom John was to work a few years later, remembers the church well: 'The beauty, ideals and creativity involved there were unique.' The woodwork had been enriched by a

THESE SAMPLES OF FOWLER'S painting show to perfection his skill with a brush. Executed quickly and with a lightness of touch they exactly capture that spirit of fantasy evident in the best of this kind of work.

10

local decorative painter, the Marquis d'Oisy, who had also devised the rather bold apple-green stairs for Lady Warwick's home nearby. Around the altar banners of deep red and pink silk were arranged and green curtains were hung to the floor within the nave's arches. There was a pale green carpet and on the altar bunches of country flowers in little glass bowls, with bright orange and yellow nasturtiums in late summer. At Christmas, plain fir trees between the arches transformed the interior into an enchanted grove.

After two short abortive jobs, with a printer in Kingston-upon-Thames and at an estate agents' office in St James', he left very disheartened for the country. He then spent a year on his cousin's small

ABOVE: THE PAINTING STUDIO behind 6 Smith Street, Chelsea. All the messy work such as stripping old furniture and rubbing down was, weather permitting, done outside in the yard. Bianca Minns (left) and Gwen Gervis are here hard at it for 10 shillings a week.

ABOVE RIGHT: THE RENTED cottage at Maytham, Kent, from the back. John Fowler working on a Spanish chair with Bianca Minns deep in concentration.

farm in Kent, where he loved working with his hands in the soil and tending the farm animals. There all sorts of early tastes were shaped, particularly a love of gardens and a preference for the simple life. Almost ten years later he was to rent a white clapboard cottage, again in Kent, where many of these influences were given expression.

The next notable event at this time was his job with Thornton Smith, a well-known firm of commercial decorators in Soho Square. This was apparently engineered by his mother, and it was here that he gained his first practical experience in the skills and techniques of decorative painting. He must have had a natural facility for the work, for he was soon taught the delicate skill of restoring old Chinese wallpapers, then much in vogue, as well as painting new facsimiles. Having attracted the attention of Margaret Kunzer, the antique dealer and decorator, he then moved on to work for her. He now painted and restored furniture, bric-à-brac, tin trays and lacquer, mostly found in the Soho and Caledonian markets. Dilapidated pieces of early nineteenth-century painted furniture in beech and pine arrived in the studio from a Suffolk dealer. Margaret Kunzer also travelled a good deal throughout northern Europe buying old painted Continental pieces as well as new sets of chairs. All these were subsequently repaired, restored and sold. Her principal client was Peter Jones and, in

1931, she was asked to set up a painting studio for them. She accepted and John Fowler, at the age of twenty-five, was appointed its head at a salary of £4 a week.

At Peter Jones, with a staff of six, the work continued apace, painting furniture, screens, wallpapers and even an off-white piano, decorated with musical motifs, for Lady Diana Cooper. In 1934, having been painting for a living for eight continuous years, John Fowler decided to resign from his job there. With him went practically all his faithful team – Gwen Gervis, Bianca Minns, Jean Hornak, Joyce Shears and Anne Talbot – all of whom would continue to work for him for many years.

This was the most important step of his life, as he was now to set up his own painting studio at Smith Street, Chelsea, round the corner from his rented terrace house in the King's Road. In the autumn of that same year, John Beresford Fowler opened shop at 292 King's Road as a decorator. Muriel Hourigan was taken on to manage the bookkeeping and secretarial work which she did from the kitchen draining board, Joyce Shears cut out and made up the curtains and Gwen Gervis's nanny did the sewing. To begin with, most of the income derived from the painting studio, which already had an established reputation, and the rooms of 292 were done up and furnished to exhibit the range of Fowler's ideas. It was a hand-to-mouth existence, with the whole enterprise run as a sort of co-operative.

From the time of his joining Thornton Smith to his leaving Peter Jones, Fowler's taste had been developing. Having started his London life with his mother in Bedford Park, an area with middle-class artistic overtones, he later moved to rooms in the King's Road to be on his own. In Chelsea, he affected a rather spirited Bohemian appearance with long hair, bow ties, floppy shirts, sandals and wide canvas trousers. The house was always full of people and, at the instigation of his old friend Frank Bennett from Peter Jones days, parties were frequent. Through him Fowler was introduced to a whole circle of new people, including artists, playwrights, actors and musicians, some of whom would become close friends and clients, such as the Sitwell brothers, Michael and Rachel Redgrave and Laurence Olivier. This

THE WHITE CLAPBOARD cottage at Maytham – as pretty and stylized as a stage set.

JOHN FOWLER AND LEWIS WAY swimming in one of the Romney Marsh dykes near the Maytham cottage. Lewis Way provided the financial backing which enabled Fowler to set up on his own at 292 King's Road, Chelsea.

FOWLER'S CURTAIN DESIGN FOR what is now the Colefax & Fowler boardroom at Brook Street. The difficult arrangement of windows includes one central narrow window flanked by a pair of wider ones. The ease of this quick sketch is a testament to his assurance when drawing or painting.

ROBE POLONAISE, ENGLISH, 1775-80. The festoon skirt was very popular for informal dress at the time. The flounces, the *choux* and the ruched bands at the sleeves are all details that Fowler used in his designs for curtain draperies.

was a period of huge assimilation for him. He played the spinet sufficiently well to play on a collection of early instruments at a house in Cheyne Walk belonging to Major Benton Fletcher, and he particularly loved the music of Vivaldi, Scarlatti and Bach. The ballet and the theatre absorbed him too; their influence was always strong and is just discernable in the more polished style of his early interiors.

Throughout his life, John Fowler displayed a rare capacity for absorbing information on all manner of subjects, which he later re-assembled into a form that he could use in his work. From early on, he was consumed by a passion for French history and art which was to remain a constant source of inspiration. It was not the formal planning or the grand conception of French interiors that appealed to him, but rather the lightness of line, and the exquisite discipline of the furniture, colours and painting techniques. He spent many hours in the various departments of the Victoria and Albert Museum, which became, in the true spirit of the founder's intentions, his university. Apart from the furniture and the paintings he studied there, he was also fascinated by the collection of period costume. Much of his later inspiration for cushions, curtains and bed draperies derived from these costumes. For example, the ruffled taffeta curtains for Mrs David Bruce, the American Ambassador's wife, in the 1950s can be traced to the finishing on the hem of an eighteenth-century costume on display there. Antique shops were a parallel source of learning, but what attracted his eye and interest did not on the whole conform to the popular taste of the time.

Fowler's painting of furniture and restoring of screens, lacquer and Chinese wallpaper had given him first-hand experience of the skill

A MORE UNUSUAL *TOILE DE* Jouy designed to create a print room effect.

FOWLER'S SKETCH FOR THE Yellow Room's curtains at 39 Brook Street. Although ropes and tassels were later added and the rosettes abandoned, the finished effect is very close to this drawing.

and facility of the eighteenth- and early nineteenth-century decorative painters. There was a lightness and freshness, as well as a spirit of exuberance, to their work which was quite different from the seriousness of the antique furniture that was being collected at that time. Most of these decorated pieces, though, were considered provincial, and it was perhaps this quality that endeared them to him. Very soon he began to buy and collect a whole range of things, some of which he used in his decorating. Whereas established taste cherished ormolu, he chose *tôle*. Serious antique dealers stocked Queen Anne walnut and carved mahogany Chippendale; he sought the Regency painted chair or the blond wood Biedermeier commode. They chose porcelain; he chose pottery or creamware. While people were still furnishing their rooms with silk damask, John Fowler was using *toile de Jouy*, plain-coloured fabrics and striped cottons. The originality of his style was already emerging, but to understand its impact it has to be seen in the context of interior decoration at this time.

In the mid 1930s the approach to decoration was becoming much more diverse and there were a number of schools of thought resulting in much debate and competition. This diversity appears to have begun soon after the First World War, when so much else was in a state of cultural flux. The pre-war period in England had been one of artistic ossification; the great age of Classicism was drawing to a close. Much of the institutional architecture was impressive, but on a domestic level the majority taste took comfort in a range of old English historical styles. In both public and private buildings interior decoration was, with a few notable exceptions, of secondary importance. Lutyens, whom most would regard as the foremost English architect of the period, produced interiors that are barely memorable except architecturally. The great houses looked shabby as their owners regarded the subject of redecoration with distaste. By and large, it was not the done thing to discuss one's house or its contents; it existed in fact and that was an end to it. Those houses that were spruced up were

ABOVE: 292 KING'S ROAD, December 1937. This profusion of pattern in a Regency context would have been beyond most people's experience at this time. A 'showroom' atmosphere still persists as Fowler had not yet learnt how to make formal rooms comfortable.

ABOVE RIGHT: THE TOP FLOOR at 292 King's Road, 1934. Here, his love of simple things is very much in evidence: Leeds creamware, pottery with printed decoration, plain and striped fabrics and matting on bare boards.

either painted pale 'Georgian' green or alternatively cream enriched with oil-gilded decoration applied to the detail – a fate that befell many fine Adam interiors at the time.

It was against this background that people were casting around for ideas. The Omega workshops were inspired by the exhilarating colours and vigorous expressionism of Matisse and the Fauves, but this movement was an intellectual affront to all but the informed and the 'artistic', and, therefore, attracted few followers. Others found that the Utopian ideals of the International Style offered a freedom from the stagnation that the old values seemed to represent. The clean white spaces, like a breath of fresh air, inspired the pure forms of Art Moderne lacquer, glass and steel that were beginning to emerge in the late 1920s. The Bauhaus architects, who created this style, did have a certain international influence: there were avant garde decorators in every major capital to whom it appealed on some level. Syrie Maugham, whose work was noted by John Fowler partly because she lived opposite him in the King's Road, was the most talented of the London exponents, although the followers of London's other modernist decorator Betty Joel might argue the point. Not only were Syrie Maugham's rooms painted white, but she also 'pickled' both old and new furniture to a point where the original colour of wood was barely discernable. But it was perhaps the boldness of her approach, more than the means she used to achieve her keen sense of style, that impressed the young Fowler. Experiment was in the air.

In traditional decoration things were changing more slowly. The taste for late seventeenth- and early eighteenth-century furniture set in period panelled rooms reflected more caution. The conservative influence of people like Margaret Jourdain, the foremost authority on English furniture, and Lord Duveen's favourite decorator, Sir Charles Allom, ensured that the stiff and rather bland approach towards the furnishing of grander homes prevailed. It was about as relaxed as having to wear Lloyd George's shirt collar during a heatwave.

Up until 1934, John Fowler's experience had been confined to painting in its various forms and decorating his own rooms in Chelsea. Now he was poised to make his own contribution to the field of interior decoration. In the front garden, outside 292, he set up a mobile shop window, a contraption half way between a wheelbarrow and vitrine, in which he displayed the wares of his trade. One week it might be a painted chair with some fabric draped across it, a lamp on a stand or a china figurine; another week it might be an upholstered chair or a table prettily set with one or two decorative pieces.

The house itself had great atmosphere, but was in a state of considerable disrepair. Apart from some exceedingly dangerous wiring, which frequently hissed and popped, its interior had probably changed little since it was occupied by noble French refugees at the end of the eighteenth century. In Fowler's time, the rooms were redecorated and, as the days shortened, the fires would be lit, the fragrance of burning juniper would fill the rooms and the candlelight

BIANCA MINNS'S DELIGHTFUL painting of the top floor at 292 King's Road. This is the country style with which Fowler felt most at ease.

16

from chandeliers and sconces would offer their own welcome to the evening's visitors. The old, uneven plaster walls were painted in coats of dead flat chalky distemper, memorably pale green in one room, cyclamen and faded coral in others.

In the low-ceilinged attic rooms the plain board floors were covered with mats of Norfolk rush. Into these rooms he put painted country furniture, pottery and plates with early nineteenth-century printed decoration. There was a wing armchair in linen, a striped cotton-covered sofa and a mass of plants producing a mood that was both light and informal. The colours were fresh and reflected the spirit of the country look with which he personally felt most comfortable.

The first floor showrooms were taller, with a proper sense of scale, decent chimney-pieces and cornices and in them he displayed more sophisticated Regency furniture. His introduction to the Regency period had come about when he was restoring such pieces for Margaret Kunzer. Later, at Peter Jones, he had seen the enthusiasm with which such furniture had been received by some of their more stylish clients. Brighton Pavilion had been a great revelation to him; he was impressed by the quality of workmanship and the rakish overtones of such studied fantasy strongly appealed to him. Hardy Amies remembers John taking many of his friends there and the book *The Regent and His Daughter* by Cresta Dormer became compulsory reading. In the front showroom a pair of early nineteenth-century tables were set either side of the chimney-piece and Regency wall sconces were put up in an altogether more formal and serious mood.

In spite of the flowers that filled the top rooms at 292, and the profusion of mauve and white striped petunias in his summer window boxes, Fowler found that he missed the country and all that it meant to him. So he rented a small cottage at Maytham, in Kent, to be used at weekends. Bianca Minns's description of the train journey there

THE FIRST-FLOOR SHOWROOM at 292 King's Road, December 1937. Fowler's flirtation with the well-mannered formality of the Regency style is very obvious. The curtain valance and tails seem to borrow more from 1930s dress fashions than from nineteenth-century curtains.

evokes a mood that is more reminiscent of one of Monet's paintings of the Gare St Lazare than of any more recent event. 'Weekends at the cottage' she recalls, 'began with a Friday night dash to Victoria Station. Fowler, the *New Statesman* tucked under his arm, gave a tip out of all proportion to his salary to a faithful porter, who then carried his white vellum suitcase and a wicker basket filled to the brim with delicious provisions, to a seat already reserved for him. To reach our destination we all completed the journey in a vaulted railway carriage wallpapered in white with tiny black stars, its iron seats covered in fringed velvet of brownish green. From the station we pushed our luggage to the cottage in a wheelbarrow.'

THE TWO-UP, TWO-DOWN cottage at Maytham, with its tiny attic rooms, had once been two farm workers' cottages, each of miniature scale.

The cottage was tiny, but had been conceived as an exquisite exercise in rustic charm. It was painted out in distemper and had simple furniture, either painted or oak, and objects of the most rural kind, wooden bowls, pottery, slipware and baskets. Friends, as well as one or two girls from the studio, remember hilarious weekends, large lunch parties with food in abundance, swimming nude in the nearby dyke, picnics and getting drunk on local cider. The garden, in which there were periods of ferocious activity, was equally important. Country flowers, wild varieties, such as sweet rocket, and herbs would all be mixed in what was to be a forerunner of his more elaborate garden at the Hunting Lodge. Plums, damsons, apples, flowers in summer and kindling wood in winter would all be loaded into baskets and hampers and, groaning under the weight, the party would return to London on Sunday afternoons.

In the late 1920s Acton Surgay had exerted a strong influence on decoration in England. His work, with its medieval/Spanish overtones, was very much to the fore as he was accustomed to taking full page advertisements in *Country Life* to promote his style. He had also regularly used the services of Thornton Smith in his work. Fowler was obviously aware of this fashion and his liking for it was in evidence in the large seventeenth-century Spanish leather chair, as well as the Spanish *torchères* and wall sconces, in his London house. He was also drawn to the medieval and had installed a stripped oak door with a latch on the top floor in London; in addition, he owned a number of pieces of rustic oak. The decoration and choice of furniture in his country cottage largely owe their origins to the Arts and Crafts Movement, which still exerted a pull on the popular imagination. This tradition had been maintained by a number of architects, amongst whom were Baillie Scott and Harrison Townsend. There was also a fashion for restoring medieval and Tudor structures as well as for collecting furniture and objects of the period. Vita Sackville-West and Gertrude Jekyll were both exponents of this style. John Fowler admired Miss Jekyll's work and was familiar with her ideas as he occasionally stayed with a neighbour of hers in Surrey.

Fowler's style was in no way dour, nor did it have any of those porridge tones that were so much in favour. His years of painting had not only given him a taste for colour, but had also taught him to use it with great sensitivity. He chose *toile de Jouy* fabrics because of their provincial charm and he used them on the pelmets in his showroom and, more liberally, in his bedrooms in London and in the country. Jean Hornak remembers the Maytham bedroom as an immensely pretty room, with the bed hung in a lilac-coloured *toile* on an off-white ground, edged in cerise.

A few years earlier, Fowler had been influenced by the Hon Mrs Guy Bethell, whom he regarded as the best decorator of her generation and with whom he had plans to work had she not died prematurely. The contribution that she made to his developing style was principally in the design of her curtains and their draperies, which were recognized as being the best of their time. In the absence of any other experienced mentor, Fowler was largely forced to turn to his own resources. In his desire to refine his skills, he took old curtains apart, studying them minutely, and experimented, with Joyce Shears, in the cut and the hang of new pairs.

The most revealing example of his work from this early period is a London drawing room furnished in 1936. Here the Regency-style

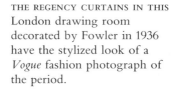

THE REGENCY CURTAINS IN THIS London drawing room decorated by Fowler in 1936 have the stylized look of a *Vogue* fashion photograph of the period.

19

curtains have the stylized look of a *Vogue* fashion photograph. Although their design is evocative of the period and the fabrics, colours and trimmings are elegant, the overall effect is rather rigid. His lack of experience shows in the build-up of his decoration. There is a strange imbalance between the architecture, the pictures and the furnishings; the spaces between the elements are not yet comfortable. This hesitancy, producing a somewhat stilted effect, may have been a response to the fashionable minimalist tendencies of Syrie Maugham and Betty Joel, who advocated the elimination of all unnecessary detail. For whatever reason, his style at this juncture had not yet arrived at the more historical approach that he was ultimately to take, and which was to prove so successful.

While he was still refining his simplified Regency style, Fowler embarked on his first trip to Paris. As this was his first taste of foreign travel, the visit made the most enormous impression on him. The decorative objects that he found in the flea markets – fragments of eighteenth-century fabrics, the lanterns and bits of china – excited him. He was impressed with the French use of paint, and intrigued by their distinctive colour palette of greys, mauves, putty off-whites, sharp yellows, blues, orange-reds and the bluer grey-reds. Although he had always collected illustrations and postcards of paintings, furniture and architecture and had almost total recall of books he had read, he found the actual experience of France breathtaking.

It was also on this trip that he came across the firm of Mauny producing wallpapers of a very special sort. This firm was to be of great importance to his future work. It had been started in 1933 and

MRS JOAN DENNIS'S BEDROOM in Hay's Mews, Mayfair. The curtains hang behind a false pelmet over which the Mauny paper border runs. This very unarchitectural device was a throwback to Fowler's pre-war days. The shaped pelmet is something he later developed for Pauline de Rothschild for the master bedroom in her Albany set with great success.

FOWLER WAS SO DETERMINED to get the proportion of this Hay's Mews room right that, just before its completion, he called a stop and insisted that the ceiling be lowered by six inches.

produced papers by hand-block printing. The pigments of the papers are thick and dry with a quality that is identical to the early nineteenth-century originals. The designs are derived mostly from the nineteenth century and range from neo-Classical motifs and small patterns to romantic floral papers.

Fowler had long had an obsession with Marie Antoinette and this visit was to reinforce it. To him, she was a guiding spirit, representing all that he admired most. Her own house, the Petit Trianon, and the Hameau appealed to his sense of the romantic. His two favourite books were *Marie Antoinette* by Stefan Zweig and *An Adventure* by Miss Moberley and Miss Jourdain. The second (which was about the ghost of Marie Antoinette) became so important to him that he would repeatedly read excerpts to all who would listen. Later, he would invariably introduce into his schemes one or two pieces of French furniture, generally chairs. This was in part inspired by his romantic attachment to the court at Versailles but, more importantly, because he appreciated how the greater sophistication and delicacy of French furniture offered relief from the masculine English forms, 'adding a dash of French to a room,' as he would say.

While Fowler was experimenting with his ideas on decoration, the studio was engaged in its traditional activity of painting and restoring furniture. Much of it was Regency and so Greek key patterns, acanthus and floral garlands were added to enrich it. The furniture was then displayed and sold at 292, where it could be seen in the context of completed rooms. Both Syrie Maugham and Sibyl Colefax, living across the road and next to one another, were regular visitors and sometimes bought pieces.

With a growing clientele, Fowler soon began to take on more jobs for customers in their own homes. One woman, who had already bought several chairs and a dining table, commissioned the studio to paint a cloudy sky on the ceiling of her house in Somerset. The team were also asked by the Duchess of Marlborough to redecorate her guest rooms at Blenheim Palace, which they did using off-white linen on the walls and chintz upholstery of grey flowers on a green ground. While they were there, the team also stripped and painted existing pieces of nineteenth-century furniture, some grey and others green and white. They also contributed to the restoration of Brighton Pavilion, working in the Yellow Room where John devised handpainted *trompe l'oeil* borders for the curtains as well as decorating the Chinese fretwork panelling in the same room. Thus the work load increased and the reputation of John Beresford Fowler grew.

Lady Colefax, like her rival Syrie Maugham, approached her work very differently from John Fowler. She exploited her social connections ruthlessly to further her career as a decorator and her dinner parties at Argyll House, one of the most beautiful eighteenth-century houses in Chelsea, were legendary. This address earned itself the name 'The Lion's Corner House', because of her tendency to lionize the famous and the talented. In 1933, she started Sibyl Colefax at 29 Bruton Street in Mayfair with Peggy Ward, later Countess Munster, as a partner. Five years later, when Peggy Ward decided to retire from the business, she advised Sibyl Colefax to take on John Fowler, whom she had met in his days at Peter Jones. The offer was accepted and in 1938 a new company was established. The arrangement was that Fowler should bring with him two helpers, Joyce Shears on the upholstery side and Muriel Hourigan as his personal assistant. The Smith Street studio was disbanded, although some of the staff continued to work freelance for the new firm.

To begin with, it is unlikely that Sibyl Colefax and John Fowler were entirely sympathetic to each other's tastes in decoration. Sibyl Colefax had a more conventional approach to furnishing houses, while Fowler was still inclined to experiment and break new ground. He was not prepared to limit his contribution to arranging furniture, designing curtains, lampshades and supplying plain Wilton wall-to-wall carpeting. As the partnership developed, he gained greater access to more important houses where he was impressed by their owners' respect for tradition. As a result, his style soon moved towards a form that was more sympathetic to this attitude.

The photograph, taken in 1939, of his first-floor sitting room, that used to be his old showroom, shows this development. His interest in Regency decoration is here more firmly established: the swagged and tailed curtain drapery, with its blocked fringe and *choux*, is much more

THE HALL IN ARGYLL HOUSE, King's Road, Chelsea. In this painting by Sir John Lavery, Sibyl Colefax is standing on the stairs talking to her great rival and neighbour Syrie Maugham. Both were in the habit of 'nipping' across the road to see what John Fowler was up to at 292.

assured and elegant. The small nineteenth-century patterned chintz, used on the pair of armchairs, indicates his growing interest in this fabric. The bowed and tasseled two-toned rope from which the portrait hangs is quite assertive, although the height at which Claudius Caesar is hung in relation to the portrait seems uncomfortable. Equally, the tiny pictures in the recess, and the absence of any others of similar scale, reflect a lack of balance.

Most of Sibyl Colefax's and John Fowler's early work together, such as Sir Alfred Beit's house in Kensington and Send Grove in Surrey, the country house of Countess Munster, no longer survives.

TWO OF THE FIRST-FLOOR rooms at 292 King's Road, as they were in June 1939. His interest in Regency decoration is now firmly established, although the odd country chair has found its way into the scheme. His decoration is more relaxed and comfortable than previously (see pages 15 and 17).

THE MAIN GUEST BEDROOM IN A West Country farmhouse. The endearing quality of this room is established by the strange proportion of its components, for example the very wide but fanciful pelmet and the tubby chest of drawers.

However, one of the last jobs that John Fowler carried out in this pre-war period, was a West Country farmhouse. Today these interiors still remain very much as they were on completion. The master bedroom is a clear distillation of his ideas and taste at the time. This beautiful room relies totally on a balance of colour, pattern and fantasy. Its effect is achieved without the aid of a single picture, a good piece of antique furniture or any architectural presence. Today, these 'extras' would be considered absolutely essential for a room to be successful.

The bedroom walls are papered with a *trompe l'oeil* Mauny design representing a pale grey draped fabric hung from cloakpins, over a pink ground. Tails of foliage, hung at intervals, echo the mossy green pattern of the Brussels weave carpet. The principal fabrics are a vermilion silk and a fine white muslin hung over pink cotton. The curtains have a viridian green and white block silk fringe and the braid to the bed valance is purple. The muslin drapes from the corona above the bed head have gathered frills. French pink opaline lamps like large crocuses sit on a pair of bedside tables. The balance of colours, with their abstract disposition in the room, is striking, and well illustrate the purity of his talent.

The main guest bedroom, in tones of gold with off-white curtains trimmed in blue, is charming and quiet. Yellow and blue rope with

23

matching rosettes give an accent of colour that lifts this otherwise restrained scheme. The yellow and white striped paper gives it the air of a tiny Regency bedroom that one might have expected to find in Brighton a century earlier.

When war was declared, Fowler, who was exempt from the services for reasons of delicate health and myopia, enlisted as a fire warden in Chelsea; Sibyl Colefax joined the Women's Voluntary Services in Belgravia. Muriel Hourigan and Lady Colefax's young assistant ran the shop, with Fowler coming in on his one day off a week.

In 1944 the offices moved from Bruton Street, where they had been since Fowler joined, to 39 Brook Street, Mayfair. This house had been the home of the nineteenth-century architect Sir Jeffry Wyattville who is remembered for his complete remodelling of Windsor Castle for George IV. Work continued at a very slow pace during this period and great ingenuity had to be used to accomplish anything at all. Strict rationing affected almost all the materials needed for their work and this state of affairs continued to make life difficult for a good five years after the war ended.

To compensate for these restrictions, imaginative use was made of all available materials. Army blankets were dyed, cut up into strips and then resewn to create a striped effect for curtains. Curtains were also made out of the surplus *noile* from silk parachutes, and pyjama fabrics, book linens and the delightful purple and white striped fabric manufactured at that time for nurses' uniforms were all turned into

THE SAMPLEBOARD OF THE master bedroom in the West Country farmhouse.

THE DECORATION OF THIS bedroom relies totally on a balance of colour, pattern and fantasy. Its effect is achieved without the aid of a single picture, good piece of antique furniture or any architectural merit.

JOHN FOWLER, PHOTOGRAPHED at his desk in 39 Brook Street in 1946, every inch the professional. When this elegant reception room later became a showroom and was fitted out to display Colefax & Fowler fabrics, John moved to the floor above where he surrounded himself with such a mass of samples and trimmings that one often had some difficulty in finding him.

instant furnishing materials. People were extremely resourceful, offering old bedspreads, sheets and damask tablecloths to be dyed and turned into slip-covers or curtains. Fowler even seized upon a pretty dress belonging to one client which were soon turned into cushions for her sitting room.

After the war, Lady Colefax, who had become increasingly crippled by ill health, retired. The business was then acquired by Nancy Lancaster and this was to be the turning point in John Fowler's career.

25

CHAPTER 2

The Influence of Nancy Lancaster

NANCY LANCASTER POSING IN the Hall for Cecil Beaton.

J OHN FOWLER'S ABILITY AS A DECORATOR REACHED ITS FULL MATURITY under the influence of Nancy Lancaster, a woman with the most remarkable and assured taste. Born into a distinguished Virginian family from Albermarle County, she was educated mainly in France before coming to England in 1915 to stay with her aunt Nancy, wife of Waldorf, later second Viscount Astor. Here she found herself at the centre of a busy social milieu; Cliveden was constantly full of politicians, artists and many of the most colourful personalities in the land. Lytton Strachey noted how impressed he was by her at one such gathering, and Nancy's enthusiasm for houses, furniture and works of art quickly drew the attention of some of her aunt's friends and relations.

In 1919, she was again invited to Cliveden, this time to get over the tragic early death of her first husband. On the ship coming over she met Ronald Tree, her late husband's American cousin who had been brought up and educated in England. Soon afterwards they were married. Their first thoughts were of living in America and so they rented a house in New York from Ogden Codman, the architect who was co-author with Edith Wharton of the immensely successful book, *The Decoration of Houses*, published in the late 1890s. They then acquired Mirador, the family house in Virginia that had originally belonged to Nancy's grandfather and where she spent her summers. When they proceeded to do it up, Nancy's inclination even at this early date was to use old chintz to create a soft and faded atmosphere that must have reflected the nostalgia for the house she remembered as a child. These old Plantation houses on the tidewater had assumed an air of rundown grandeur after the strife of the civil war, and stirred in her a sympathy for a vanished way of life. She was intensely patriotic in her feeling for the South and always flew the Confederate flag over all her houses.

In 1926 the Trees returned to England. First they leased Cottesbrooke, in Northamptonshire, then Kelmarsh Hall, in the same county. Just before the war they moved to Ditchley Park, in Oxfordshire, which they bought lock, stock and barrel – the house, a 3,000 acre estate and practically all of its contents – not such an uncommon practice in those days. Both Kelmarsh and Ditchley were built by one of the great eighteenth-century English architects, James Gibbs. It was Nancy Lancaster's outstanding and sympathetic restoration and decoration of these two important houses and their gardens that earned

OPPOSITE: THE ENTRANCE HALL at Haseley Court, Oxfordshire, with an amusing mixture of things: croquet mallets, a red dog basket matching the curtains and window seat and a pig boot brush, wayward amongst such well-born surroundings.

her such acclaim in the years before the war. During the war, Winston Churchill and his staff used to stay at Ditchley at those times of the full moon when Chequers was considered vulnerable to enemy bombing. After the war, the Trees' marriage ended and Nancy was briefly married to Claude Lancaster, the owner of Kelmarsh, to which they both returned for a while.

When John Fowler met Nancy Lancaster he was still on the threshold of his career. She, on the other hand, had an established reputation as a superb hostess and a beauty of her day. Her connections with the aristocracy and the smart county hunting set were worlds apart from anything that Fowler had known in his own social background. She was familiar with the great houses and loved the life that went on within them. To her, houses should be brimming with activity and exhilarating in spirit – and this she had no difficulty in achieving.

In 1954, after much arduous searching, she found Haseley Court in Oxfordshire, in a state of near dereliction. She and John Fowler then embarked on the most remarkable collaboration in the restoration of this house and transformed it into a place of such rhythmical beauty, wit and comfort that it must stand as a paragon of its kind. After all the important houses Nancy Lancaster had lived in, Haseley might have appeared less promising, but she saw its potential. This

THE HALL AT HASELEY, WITH its glorious Palladian chimney-piece. The furniture is tough and matches the room's strong architectural mood. Brackets and busts, together with the garniture of blue and white Delft, relieve the room's severity.

eighteenth-century house had been subjected to various periods of change and from three sides it looked a jumble. Once the Victorian additions had been discreetly removed, they left a house that had considerable variety and surprise. There was an early Georgian core, with compact, smaller rooms, flanked by two larger rooms, the early nineteenth-century Gothic Revival Library on one side and the neo-Classical Saloon rising through two stories on the other.

At first glance, the completed decoration appears to have all the characteristics of an eighteenth- or early nineteenth-century house. This, however, is not the case as it lacks the strict uniformity for which contemporary architects and owners strove. In those days the furniture is likely to have been *en suite* and the choice of furnishing fabrics kept to a minimum. Here the approach is very different. The house presents us with a well-used and handed-down look that is the very antithesis of historical correctness. It is as if its original form has largely been lost sight of as succeeding generations have changed things around to suit their convenience; as if a life of easy and charmed informality has prevailed over correctness and house parties have succeeded musical evenings and balls. It is the victory of the imagination over scholarship. This does not mean that the way its decoration evolved is haphazard; it is in fact an expression of pure creativity, with all the authority and discipline that one would expect of a fine building. However, the rules are more difficult to recognize because the play of intuition and invention has disguised them.

NANCY PHOTOGRAPHED BY Cecil Beaton on the terrace. She sits regally with the topiary in the garden behind looking like an army of attendant servants.

THE DINING ROOM: AN essentially masculine room softened by chintz slip-covers on a pair of wing chairs, the chintz matching that of the curtains.

In the Hall, the hand-painted cover of blue and white pots belonging to the Queen Anne chair echoes the blue and white Delft garniture on the monumental stone chimney-piece. A second Queen Anne needlework wing chair, also with a design of pots on a red ground, and two huge Delft *tulipières*, standing sentinel on either side of the console table, complete the main theme of the room. The red-painted dog basket in front of the red curtains and window seat impertinently jostles for attention. Other touches of humour are found in the pig bootbrush, so out of place in these well-born surroundings, and in the carved wooden dog and the dressed-up brush, looking like discarded toys. The stone-coloured paintwork on the walls has been applied with an open technique which is sympathetic to the stone paving and chimney-piece; it establishes a neutral background for some of the richer effects in the rooms beyond.

The Dining Room, with its warm panelling painted in pale biscuit, its black leather single chairs and black lacquer furniture set on a rich Heriz rug, has a strong masculine presence. In contrast, the busy chintz used on the curtains, window seats and wingchair covers enlivens the mood. The gloriously romantic epergne for sweetmeats and flowers stands poised like a dancing girl beneath the chandelier. At night, when the curtains are drawn, the mirror gives the view of the whole room lit by the flickering chandelier.

The Palladian Room, used as a card room, has a hand-painted Chinese wallpaper based on an eighteenth-century paper seen and admired by Nancy in Drottninghölm Castle. The King of Sweden,

BOTTOM LEFT: THE PALLADIAN Room at Haseley, with its handpainted wallpaper executed by George Oakes and based on a facsimile of an eighteenth-century paper at Drottninghölm Castle which the King of Sweden had especially reproduced for Nancy Lancaster.

BELOW: THE DECORATION IN the Library at Haseley is strong, deep-toned and masculine to balance the ethereal quality of the neo-Classical saloon (opposite) at the other end of the house.

THE SALOON RISES majestically through two stories. A haphazard arrangement of comfortable furniture has been organized around the strong central axis created by a large upholstered sociable and an extremely fine English chandelier that hangs directly above it.

sensing her enthusiasm, instructed his conservators to make a copy which she brought home. This wallpaper was painted by George Oakes, a young artist who was just beginning his career with John Fowler. The ground colour has been darkened and distressed and the tones greyed in order that the picture, black with age, and the French chairs, in their slightly scruffy original paint, should look in place. The leaf pattern of the 'Blind Earl' plates on the shelves repeat the wallpaper's design in a pleasing way. The French chairs in their old blue *toile* covers and the short tablecloth of stamped velvet are a seemingly careless mix, giving this small room a charmingly intimate atmosphere which contrasts well with the grandeur of the Saloon.

The Saloon is a magnificent double-height room, the main element being a neo-Classical ceiling enriched with circles and swags of husks and medallions. In the planning, a formal arrangement has been abandoned for a pleasing jumble of comfortable chairs, skirted tables and fine antiques. The only acknowledgement to order is the large upholstered sociable, ruched, tufted and skirted in the palest sea-green silk, centred beneath the chandelier. The room's gossamer tones, from

31

the soft blue-green of the silk walls, the chintz and yellows of the furniture to the huge faded acanthus scrolls of the Aubusson carpet, are like the bleached colours of summer. The architecture is sharpened by the use of burnished gold. Gilt bands on the ceiling and fillets to the edges of the walls answer the gilt of the looking glasses, picture frames and carved tendrils of the *girandoles*. This, above all, is a 'lived-in' room, one that is loved and used to the full.

The large Library at the other end of the house is warm, enveloping and masculine. It is perfect for evening use and the mellow browns, reds and greens reflect the colours of the books. The grand piano and the brown furniture are all set on the red 'Roses and Ribbons' carpet which completes the mood. The curtains to the bay windows have ingeniously devised false pelmets, fringed under the pole. When closed, their elaborate swags provide the enrichment, while, during the day, all is swept aside. Although it is not shown in the illustration here, there was sometimes an eight-foot-high laburnum tree standing on the piano, its yellow fronds looking exquisite against the background of beige and brown.

The Tobacco Bedroom is in tones of white, almost a laundered white, and brown. The whole scheme, however, is subordinate to the most exotic sepia scenic wallpaper by Dufour based on the popular eighteenth-century romance *Paul et Virginie*. Set against this background are a nineteenth-century bed, with antique white cotton hangings edged with a pretty mimosa fringe, and the 'Roses and Ribbons' Brussels carpet, both acquired at the Ashburnham Place sale a year or so earlier. The bed's quilt and the curtains, with a gathered and fringed pelmet, are also white, as is the dressing table, the china and the amusingly untidy lampshade by the fireplace looking like a housemaid's pinny.

Comfortable chairs and a table are placed by the fire, ready for a guest's breakfast; every comfort catered for. The small design of the chintz, in brown and yellow on a cream ground, is exactly right: while not detracting from the paper, the pattern adds interest to the decoration and ties in with the colours of the carpet and the tones of the paintwork. This is a room 'a man could be happy in', as Mrs Bruce observed when she first saw the room.

The Gothic Bedroom was initially decorated for Nancy herself, but it was later used by Nancy Astor. This princely room is dominated by the tall *lit à la Polonaise* that stands upon a dais like a royal bier borne high above an enchanted garden. The room was completely altered from its original sombre Gothic state with its stained dado panelling and boarded ceiling. It was lightened and its Gothic Revival overtones now speak of the eighteenth century. The walls, the eaves and the ceiling are painted in a huge *trompe l'oeil* design of panels, medallions and swags of oak leaves in *grisaille* on two tones of burnt orange. This was painted to look like plaster. The oyster silks on the furniture and bed echo the *grisaille* decoration and the pale green silk gives counterpoint. The swastika pattern on the early Georgian needlework carpet, with its huge central sunflower design, provides pattern of exactly the right scale and colour.

THE GOTHIC BEDROOM, painted by George Oakes and John Fowler to look like *grisaille* decoration on plaster. Nancy complained that John's portrayal of Diana the Huntress above the chimney-piece showed that he did not understand female anatomy very well.

NANCY LANCASTER'S STRAW hats under the stairs, a metaphor for her throw-away style.

THE GOTHIC BEDROOM WAS THE principal spare bedroom. The *lit à la Polonaise* stands upon a dais high above the rest of this most romantic bedroom. The geometry of the ceiling makes this room seem like some fantastic tent from the 'Field of the Cloth of Gold'.

It was in the creation of this house, where he worked so closely with Nancy Lancaster, that John Fowler learned the lessons that he was able to put to such good use later in his career. There is little doubt that, although his skill in painting rooms and creating the correct effects in curtains and upholstery contributed much, the basic driving force was hers. The choice of furniture and the conception of these rooms reflect a strength of purpose and a level of imagination that must have been quite new to him.

Fine interiors with elaborate plasterwork, sculptured overdoors and a profusion of carved detail did not intimidate her as they might those new to the experience. She understood how magnificent furniture, chandeliers and a wealth of possessions could enhance the charm of life. At the same time there was an edge to her talent which inclined her to irreverence. She had what Cecil Beaton referred to as a 'healthy disregard for the sanctity of "important" pieces'. She could put the ordinary and appealing beside the grand and imposing so that the overall effect was totally unpretentious. It was this self-confidence which, combined with John Fowler's eye for tone, texture and detail,

resulted in Haseley becoming the apotheosis of the Colefax & Fowler style. Nancy Lancaster had an insatiable curiosity, with an ability to recognize, in furniture and objects, the inspired as distinct from what was just good. She assembled her rooms with a wit and vibrance that matched her own personality, and she had star quality. A perfect sense of scale was fundamental to her talent, and in large spaces this is of the greatest importance. Once the decoration was complete, she then humanized it, making it comfortable with small touches, wonderful china and flowers. The flowers in her rooms were as glorious as those in her gardens and into these she channelled infinite love and care. Husbands she liked; houses she liked more, 'they last,' as she pointed out; but perhaps she liked gardens most of all.

There were other, more pragmatic, aspects to Nancy Lancaster's style of living that were unusual in large houses at that time. English country houses were often large, drafty and ill-lit. They had little or no central heating and plumbing of the most curious sort. The bathrooms were large, bleak rooms with linoleum floors and baths that ran five minutes of rust-red water for the first occupant. The ratio of bathrooms to bedrooms resulted in some arduous games early in the mornings, with disappointment or frustration for all but the nimble. Nancy Lancaster's arrangements were quite different. She devised *en suite* bathrooms for all her guests and even made sure her staff were well cared for. Guest bathrooms were furnished like small studies: they were carpeted and had pretty needlework rugs, small armchairs, chests of drawers, china, books, prints and paintings on the walls. Comfort was of the highest priority and every sort of item a guest might have forgotten to pack was provided from Floris sandalwood essence to cosmetics – and even an occasional log fire.

The bedrooms certainly had fires and each was furnished like a sitting room with all possible needs anticipated: a carafe of fresh water, flowers, books, a notepad, pencils and a telephone were all placed within easy reach of the bed. Today, people may be surprised by these observations, since standards of hospitality have risen. But in the 1950s and 1960s this was far from the case. The Duke of Beaufort, a great friend of Nancy Lancaster's, says: 'Nancy had great flair, a knack for doing up houses that is American. She had a sybaritic taste; being a sybarite, I like that!' The American influence on this aspect of the English country house style has been profound.

Both she and John Fowler liked the ease and comfort that comes from a degree of informality. Rooms should look as if they have been used and enjoyed and therefore carry the patina of life. He was able to achieve the effect in paint as well as in the dyeing of his fabrics and the restrained restoration of antique furniture. She appreciated this but was even more cavalier, especially if things were too new. Her 'bashing about', upon which she would then embark, meant taking a sofa into the garden to let the rain fall on it and letting the sun bleach the loose-cover material. She even washed chintz in tea to give it an aged look – all this was done so that people could put their feet up and relax in surroundings that looked well-used. On the other hand, the highest standards were maintained: her tables boasted crisp white damask

OPPOSITE AND ABOVE: THE Tobacco Bedroom, with its scenic wallpaper by Dufour based on a popular eighteenth-century romance. The bed, the drapes and the dressing table are all pure white against a background of browns and warm greys. The Brussels weave carpet is the original 'Roses and Ribbons' from which the Colefax design is now copied.

cloths and sparkling silver and her rooms were filled with the scent from bowls of pot-pourri and fresh-cut flowers. True luxury is the balance of comfort and perfection.

Nancy Lancaster and John Fowler both possessed remarkable powers of selective observation which they applied to just about everything they saw. They loved looking for antiques in the country, being driven off by Wilson, the chauffeur, in a huge Daimler at a majestically slow speed. They would go to country house sales where Nancy would buy things for her own homes and John, with what little there was to spend, would buy for the shop. Pieces of painted Regency furniture were still cheap, as were eighteenth-century prints and the odd Staffordshire botanical plate.

Filled with such pieces, which were being passed over by the vast majority of dealers as well as by the public, the Brook Street shop had a charming atmosphere. It had the mood of a modest country house, especially when viewed through to the huge green panoply of the catalpa tree in the courtyard beyond. The appeal of these rooms, and the influence they had on other dealers, was profound.

If Nancy Lancaster's personality was a revelation to Fowler, their partnership did not run entirely smoothly. Obviously, there were areas of deep sympathy and common interest; however, there were also differences. She was quick to conceive an overall idea and left the details to be worked out by others. She had considerable experience in using decorators, such as the Hon Mrs Guy Bethell at Kelmarsh, and Stephane Boudin at Ditchley, both considered among the best decorators of their time. She was not averse to playing the role of decorator herself on occasion and such was her authority and enthusiasm when it came to houses and their interiors that she had even been approached by various established decorators to work with them on a professional basis. Offers of partnership came from both Sibyl Colefax and her rival Syrie Maugham.

John Fowler was younger and less experienced than those she had previously worked with; besides, he had a more reflective and academic approach. He preferred to scratch around, looking, finding out, thinking, until the entire picture was brought to life in his mind. Whereas, initially, her sense of scale was much better and bolder than his, he, as the designer, understood exactly how effects could be achieved, and to him the detail and finish of things were fundamental. Because their tastes were so similar, the differences between them were highlighted, and they often became contentious. She was expansive and cajoled him with teasing; he was explosive. Nancy Astor referred to them as 'the unhappiest unmarried couple in England'. In fact, they were close and had enormous mutual respect. Nancy Lancaster was able to introduce Fowler to many of her friends and relations and they in turn became his close friends and clients. The days of being just an appendage to Lady Colefax and having to eat alone in the nursery at Petworth and to use the tradesman's entrance were now over for John Fowler.

In the late 1940s John Fowler started making regular trips to Paris again. He loved the prestige of catching the night Pullman, the Golden

ABOVE: THE LONG GALLERY AT Mereworth Castle, Kent, built to the designs of Colen Campbell in 1722. One of England's finest Palladian houses, it was the home of Nancy Lancaster's eldest son, Michael Tree.

Arrow, from Victoria and arriving at Paris in time for breakfast. This was his idea of luxury. He would then haunt the Left Bank shops bringing back, among other things, small pieces of furniture and *fauteuils*, often broken, to be repaired in the basement of the Brook Street shop. Great care was always taken to preserve the original paint, however flaky and worn. His passion for things French continued to absorb him and he made several trips to Versailles. He was spellbound by the idea of Marie Antoinette and her court playing at being peasants and it fuelled his imagination and feelings about the Hunting Lodge which he had bought a year or two before.

His mastery of the French language was poor, but he had a musical ear and his accent was very good, if somewhat exaggerated. Imogen Taylor, his assistant for many years, remembers that at this point in his life anything French was taken very seriously. One had to know

RIGHT: JOHN FOWLER IN HIS own room at 39 Brook Street surrounded by trimmings, Mauny papers and borders, as well as hundreds of dyed fabric samples.

ABOVE: THE ROTUNDA AT Mereworth after it had been painted by John Fowler.

the difference between a *bergère* and a *marquise* and to recognize a *duchesse* when the carriers delivered it to the shop. Colours also had their particular names like 'Nattier blue' or '*taupe*'. 'You fool,' he would chide a young assistant, 'don't you know what colour *taupe* is?' Amusingly, Nancy Lancaster, who had been educated in France, called a similar colour 'elephant's breath', although she also contributed to Fowler's vocabulary of French-named colours with two of her own, '*caca du dauphin*' and '*vomitesse de la reine*' – not surprisingly, spicy, natural tones that they both enjoyed using liberally.

Nancy also encouraged Fowler to broaden his horizons and recommended that he visit the Palladian villas of the Veneto. This was a great success and the benefit of this experience can be seen in his subsequent work. The colours that he so often used, both inside and outside, reflect the impression that they made on him. It is not certain that he saw the Tempietto di Maser, but the washed colours of its walls,

37

from chrome lemon yellow through to pinks, siennas and burnt oranges, seem to span what was to become his preferred architectural colour palette. He did see Andrea Palladio's Malcontenta and Rotonda, with its frescoes by Ludovico Dorigny. The garlands of flowers, the simulated marbles and *trompe l'oeil* effects in the decoration were bound to strike a chord of sympathy, but they were of a scale and daring for which he was unprepared. La Rocca Pisana, Scamozzi's masterpiece, with its graphic handling of the interior architecture, codifies the way in which Fowler was to give his interior schemes architectural definition. This can be seen in his handling of the Rotunda at Mereworth Castle, the library vestibule at Christ

Church, Oxford, and James Wyatt's cloisters at Wilton House. He had awakened to the presence of architecture.

They also went to Portugal together, where he was enchanted by the colours of the buildings around Cintra and particularly by the Palace of Queluz. The fresco painting of eighteenth-century Portuguese architecture appealed to him with its strange mix of North Italian and English decoration reminiscent of the last quarter of the eighteenth century, his favourite period.

While he was working on Haseley, Fowler was also being introduced to grander houses and stimulated by his trip to the Veneto, he was making observations about architecture and the importance of being bold with scale. How quickly he assimilated his experiences can

JAMES WYATT'S CLOISTERS AT Wilton House. The pale sienna has been stipple-painted over a yellow ground which gives vibrancy to the walls; the beds to the vaults are a paler shade of the same colour. The ribs, capitals, supporting shafts and skirting are stipple-painted a pale stone colour.

THE DECORATION OF THE Yellow Room at Avery Row was a collaboration between Nancy Lancaster and John Fowler. This most famous of London drawing rooms has all the panache of an Italian palazzo.

A BUST OF MARIE ANTOINETTE stands proudly on a wooden column at 39 Brook Street. This Regency hall, showing Wyatville's design at its most severe, benefits from the marblizing on the walls.

OVERLEAF: NANCY LANCASTER'S bedroom at Avery Row has a gloriously 'tired' quality that is more French than English.

be seen by his use of colour in interiors of the time; no longer were they employed as a subjective expression of personal preference, but they were used as a means of emphasizing the nature of the place. When it came to arranging objects and placing pictures, sconces and brackets within a room the results were much more self-assured. The slight stiffness of the Sibyl Colefax days was past; the spaces between things had become more comfortable.

It is from the middle of the 1950s and throughout the 1960s that John Fowler's full range of talents is to be seen at its best. Decoration, furniture and houses, as well as the life within them and their gardens, were his all-consuming passions and he now handled the full gamut both brilliantly and with great authority. In spite of the enormous volume of work that came with Nancy Lancaster's acquisition of the business, the profits were either non-existent or there was a deficit. Nancy had acquired Colefax & Fowler as a means of achieving the best results for herself at minimal personal expense. Nancy Astor and other relations for whom the firm now worked obtained its services on very preferential terms. John Fowler, who was the most diligent decorator ever when it came to the shape of a tassel, the scale of a gimp or the colour of a dyed ottoman silk, could not have been less interested in the business. By 1957 the firm's finances were sufficiently rocky for Barclays Bank to have been leased the ground floor of 39 Brook Street and it was decided that Nancy Lancaster should turn the saloon at the back into her 'bed-sit', as she was to call it.

The decoration of this room, once thought to have been Jeffry Wyatville's drawing office, was to be another example of Nancy Lancaster's and John Fowler's collaboration, with marvellous results. It is difficult to apportion credit, but the painting of the swagged husk decoration in the tympani above the marblized cornice, the skirting and the curtain designs appear to be Fowler's work. The basic concept, colour scheme, and composition of the furniture arranged around the walls, however, carry Nancy Lancaster's stamp.

The planning of this room establishes a balance between the sort of casual comfort that is suitable for a large present-day drawing room (and this one is 14 metres long), while paying homage to the formal treatment that traditionally belongs to such great rooms. Fowler's drapes, which embody the spirit of the late eighteenth century are grandiose and complement the architecture; the outer curtains, which are Italian-strung and made up in unlined yellow silk taffeta, are caught at the head by bows from which loosely hang two-toned ropes and tassels, in bronze-umber and yellow.

It is the scale of the wall treatment, reminiscent of an Italian palazzo, through which the formality is established. There is a pair of huge Elizabethan portraits of the Fitton sisters, and a further pair of portraits in William Kent frames are given extra scale and elegance by the silk sashes and bows from which they hang. The brilliance, however, is in the use of mirrors, which creates the illusion of even greater space. Mirrors are set into the two blind arches around the door architraves at each end of the room and into the backs of the window shutters, so that at night, with the curtains open and the shutters closed, the space becomes vast and mysterious. Four Venetian looking glasses hang over painted bookcases with Mason's ironstone pots, creating a composition which perfectly matches the scale of architecture. The practice of putting huge pots on cupboards, for which there are many eighteenth-century precedents, is often employed by decorators today; it was a rare and bold decision at the time.

A Venetian mirror, with a carved grotto frame, over the chimney-piece and three chandeliers make the choice of the glowing Italianate yellow paint of the walls seem almost inevitable. A roomful of yellows – from citrus to buttercup, gold to umber – form the back-

ground to the floral patterns of a chintz, which Fowler had specially printed, and of a beautiful Ukrainian rug. This drawing room, while Nancy used it, was always full of fresh flowers. Overlooking the secret paved garden, dominated by the sharp green of the huge catalpa tree, it was as memorable a London drawing room as has ever been seen.

Her bedroom, leading off this room, has a gloriously tired quality that is more French than English. The arrangement of the corona and bed drapes held with cloakpins is baroque; the French *faux* panelling was painted by Fowler in three tones of blue. The plain Wilton carpet is in 'mouseback', the only colour that he thought acceptable, a 'nothing' colour besides which other colours are enhanced. Nancy Lancaster chose an eclectic mixture of furniture, a pretty country chair, a French armchair in 'Berkeley Sprig' and a wonderful export bureau in *Japonaise* lacquer that echoes the pattern of the blue and white 'Moiré Stripe' chintz.

By 1975, due to a shortage of space, it became necessary to re-possess the Wyatville saloon and so Nancy Lancaster lost her apartment. About the same time, Haseley Court suffered a bad fire, so she moved to a coach house nearby.

The conversion of this building involved a major change of out-look. Her previous houses had been grand and on a scale that demanded bold treatment; these cottage spaces are the very opposite. In the former, the interiors were handled in a variety of ways, accentuating their various functions and characters. Here the rooms are all similar in mood so that the whole house emerges as a single decorative statement. The tone has been kept uniformly light; the same neutral-coloured carpet is used as a background floor covering throughout. The walls are mostly painted in warm off-whites which look as if they have been in their present state for generations. Patterned wall coverings have been used in two upstairs bedrooms, and both have the same cream-coloured ground. Because of the odd window shapes, the curtains have been treated very simply so that they match the walls and visually disappear.

What is remarkable and gives this house its personality is the structured clutter on the walls. China, paintings, drawings and prints are all beautifully composed. The blue and white plates on the walls of the drawing room pick up the blue of the Greek striped cotton fabric on the sofa and armchairs. The blue Chinese plates in the dining room

THE SITTING ROOM OF THE Coach House, Oxfordshire, has a muted colour scheme which disguises the absence of architecture and plays up the walls' decoration, which Nancy Lancaster has designed to perfection.

PREVIOUS PAGE: IT IS THE build-up of its component parts that makes the Yellow Room so masterly. The bookcases are surmounted by Mason's ironstone pots in front of Venetian mirrors. The portraits are perfect in scale as are Fowler's magnificent yellow silk taffeta curtains.

THE COACH HOUSE DINING room is grandeur on a Lilliputian scale.

reflect the rug on the floor and the 'Seaweed' chintz on the dining chairs. These plates also lend support to the shape of the giltwood mirror, as well as the *trompe l'oeil* panelling, so that the architecture and the decoration are reconciled. The wall area above the windows has been used as an opportunity for decoration, improving the proportions and adding interest to what would otherwise be an ugly space. The oval pictures forming the group behind the sofa in the drawing room have been linked by a red cord and tassels in a manner that is reminiscent of eighteenth-century print rooms.

The bedrooms have been decorated in a French style, with a single pattern covering everything. The master bedroom has an 'Angoulême' wallpaper with a matching border. The curtains, the bed and its attendant drapes have the same design printed on Irish linen. Nancy has used her own design of corona and drapes, which gives a pleasing sense of height to the bed and complements the line of the eaves. The small bound and gathered frill on the bed drapes connects prettily with the wallpaper border. The guest room, with an all-over treatment of a modern American print and cream and green painted furniture, is like a summer field.

The quality of the furniture and objects found in this house is delightful and shows her keen eye for the unusual and the witty. The rocking chair in the sitting room and the five-legged cane bedroom chair (surely the most bizarre manifestation of the chair maker's craft) are illustrations of this. The drawings, and the collection of miniatures of military gentlemen in exaggerated hats, all are a delight. These rooms are charming, comfortable, welcoming and full of amusement.

Over the years, various contributions to John Fowler's development were made by a number of people, but there is none to compare with that of Nancy Lancaster and for this we should all be grateful.

BELOW: THE SPARE BEDROOM uses a modern American print on everything in the manner of a *toile de Jouy*. The effect is of a summer field.

RIGHT: NANCY LANCASTER'S bedroom is covered in the tiny pattern 'Angoulême'. It is on the walls as a paper with a matching border and has been printed on to linen for use on the bed drapes and curtains.

<table>
<tr><td>CHAPTER 3</td><td></td></tr>
</table>

The Mature Style of John Fowler

ABOVE: THE WALLS OF THE Christ Church library are stipple-painted on Italianate pink, with a paler version taken up into the ceiling. The ribs and the plaster enrichment are painted in soft white with a most delicate picking-out in gold.

OPPOSITE: CHRIST CHURCH, Oxford. It was on this staircase that Fowler delivered his stinging retort to some startled dons who had dared to suggest a wall colour. 'If it's lingerie pink you want, well then you have come to the wrong man.'

JOHN FOWLER'S CAREER REALLY TOOK OFF IN THE EARLY 1950S AFTER Nancy Lancaster had introduced him to her circle of friends, particularly the Anglo-Americans to whom she was related. He started by working on Nancy's own Charles Street home in Mayfair, as well as for Nancy Astor in Hill Street around the corner. At Bruern Abbey, in Oxfordshire, he helped Nancy Astor's son, Michael, and later decorated for his sister, Lady Ancaster, at her two houses, Grimsthorpe Castle, in Lincolnshire, built by Vanbrugh and Drummond Castle, in Scotland. As Haseley Court was being done up at approximately the same time, he was fully occupied by a massive amount of work in houses of serious architectural content.

The Americans, with money behind them and an appreciation of comfort, presented Fowler with a unique opportunity to extend his range. The prevalent English practice of simply disguising the ravages of time, by repainting here and ordering new slip-covers there, was not at all how his new clients saw his role. They understood that decorating houses was a positive undertaking, to be carried right through a house, creating a sense of continuity and injecting new vigour. These houses required a more serious approach to decoration and this experience, to which he rose, added weight and authority to his work. It is from this period that his development moved on, from being the mere imposition of ideas by someone with a fine sense of colour in search of a canvas, to a decorator who understood that the quality of the architecture was the key to achieving the most impressive results.

Through his decorative painting, Fowler had considerable experience of using colour and tone to express the essence of a design. When it came to architecture, this was invaluable. His feeling for three-dimensional decorative form, whether enriched plasterwork or the guilloche frieze of a side table, enabled him to define detail by tonal variation without disrupting the overall effect. When applying colour to an entablature or the component parts of an elaborate door-case this sensitivity is of the greatest importance. The treatment of the architecture should make sense in all its constituent parts without detracting from the overall unity. Working in distinguished houses and with the inspiration of his trip to the Veneto, Fowler developed a distinct love of interiors with a strong architectural presence, and throughout the late 1950s and 1960s he proved that he had considerable skill in handling them. He spent time studying rooms and working out exactly how to give architectural definition by varying his tones of off-white.

Skirtings were toned to dados and in turn to chair rails, architraves and door panels; the cornice and ceiling were then related to the walls, and all these would all be reappraised so the exact balance could be struck.

LADY ANCASTER'S BEDROOM AT Grimsthorpe Castle. The restoration of the Chinese wallpaper was one of the first jobs undertaken by George Oakes when he joined John Fowler.

The library at Christ Church, Oxford, is an excellent example of his decoration of this period. The Italianate pink of the walls and the softer version of the same colour on the ceiling bed are eminently appropriate for this most Classical interior. The range of greys and off-whites act as cool counterpoint to the pinks and give emphasis to their warmth. The restrained use of gilding on the fillets, the *paterae* and the entablature's enrichment adds a crispness to the decoration. From now on, pinks, sienna and warm yellows were to form his favourite architectural palette. Portland and Bath stone look wonderful against these colours as do similar tones of stone grey and off-whites in paint. At Mereworth Castle in Kent a soft sienna was applied to the walls of the Rotunda. This colour gave emphasis to the Italian origins of this splendid, neo-Palladian English house that was directly inspired by the Villa Capra at Vicenza. He had James Wyatt's cloisters at Wilton House painted in shades of melon, and he used warm yellows in many other houses to give a richness and warmth that compensate so well for our often flat dull light.

THE DRAWING ROOM AT
Tyninghame, Lothian, with
its yellow walls, floral chintz
and Pontrimoli carpet.
Although this is a nineteenth-
century house, its decoration
gives it an air of the late
eighteenth century.

Tyninghame, in Lothian, built in the 1830s by the architect William Burn, had been unlived in for thirty years and the main rooms still had the original nineteenth-century flocked wallpapers. The atmosphere was very dour and Lady Haddington was determined to bring light and freshness into the house. The main sitting room was the best of the reception rooms, with wonderful views over the park and the sea. Fowler's decoration here is not authentic in any historical sense as it chooses to ignore the period of the house which is evident in the very wide nineteenth-century windows. His creation is a twentieth-century drawing room that has echoes of the late eighteenth century, a balance between comfort and a Classical discipline. This order is reflected in the composition of the pyramidal bookcases either side of a newly installed pedimented doorcase. The overmantle and the white marble baroque chimney-piece are in the same vein.

The colour scheme, a saturation of yellow walls and drapes, uses the tinted white paintwork, the off-white grounds of the 'Brompton Stock' chintz and the Pontrimoli carpet against which to set its glow. Other colours which are found in the chintz – salmon pink, pale grey-green, sour greens, ivory and Naples yellow – give a delightful variation to the principal colour. The air of summer celebration in this scheme is continued in the frilled profiles to the lampshades, edges to the cushions, skirts to the slip-covers and table cloth. The curtains are a glorious creation; they have over-draperies of scalloped and bound kerchiefs, swagged headings and attendant tails held by *choux* at the head. The heavy yellow corduroy is edged in a yellow and white fringe and tied back with bows; cream poplin festoon blinds are provided to control the light. At evening time, the gilt fillets and burnished detail on the over-door and over-mantle flash reflected light from the shadows. The success of this room, like so many others shown here, is a result of a complete rapport between John Fowler and the client. Lady Haddington and he became close friends, their ideas and tastes were similar and the clarity of this room is a testament to their shared perception.

In the course of his career, John Fowler worked on many houses, some modest, others the great stately homes of parade, including Chequers in Buckinghamshire, Holyroodhouse in Edinburgh and Buckingham Palace. Without doubt, his most successful decoration was carried out for people with taste, curiosity and a passionate interest in this absorbing subject. Certainly, as far as all the jobs considered here are concerned, the people themselves were as special to him as the work that he undertook on their behalf. 'One needs good architecture', as Tom Parr, who succeeded John Fowler as the principal decorator in Colefax & Fowler, once defined the problem of successful decoration, 'and the wherewithal to acquire the right furniture and pictures where and when necessary, but above all one needs a good client.'

In 1955 the Viscount Hambleden decided to celebrate his marriage to his beautiful young Italian bride by decorating his home, and it was to Colefax & Fowler that he turned. When Fowler first met Carmela, he was captivated by the personality of this patrician young woman who stood a good six inches above him. He evidently took great pleasure in working on this house for her since its decoration carries the stamp of his love of Italy and France.

The main house is an early seventeenth-century knapped flint structure with brick quions. On the back, there are some Regency additions, rooms of fine size and proportions like the drawing room illustrated here. Like so many of Fowler's best clients, Lady Hambleden collected furniture and art and the huge Aubusson carpet, around which the colours of this room are composed, was found and bought by her.

When Fowler mixed the pink and had it applied to the walls, Lady Hambleden remembers complaining that the colour was much too strong. She wanted it over-painted a paler shade as she felt she could never live with it as it was. 'No,' came the answer, 'it will fade to a terrible yellow if you start with such a light colour.' On Fowler's insistence, the pink was left as he had painted it, and, as he had foretold, within a year or two it had faded. It is now a glorious slightly uneven apricot colour and has been this way for over thirty years. The colour scheme depends on an interplay between the apricot tones of the walls, curtains and silk lampshades and the wine reds used on the Venetian open armchairs and cushion borders, which tie into the red

of the Aubusson. Complementary colours of sage and sour green give bite to the scheme.

The headings to the curtains are designed with great sweeping Regency swags and tails in apricot silk ottoman. The tops, in deeper tones, are finished with a ruched band and the bottom edges with a fringe. Lady Hambleden wished to use the existing draw curtains which were in deep red velour, so Fowler bleached them to a dirty yellowed pink – a colour that is half way between that of the walls and the stone picking-out of the ogee plaster moulding.

The seating is dominated by a huge sofa in a pale off-white damask which in winter is the focus of the room's use. In summer the scene shifts to the arrangement of banquettes and chairs in the large bay window from where one can sit and watch the sun track across the rural glades that stretch down to the Thames valley beyond. There is a

PREVIOUS PAGE: THE DRAWING room at Hambleden Manor. The colour scheme depends on an interplay between the apricot tones and the wine reds which tie into the red of the Aubusson carpet. Complementary colours of sage and sour green give it bite.

THE LITTLE VIEWS OF ROME and Naples, along with the Continental overdoor, give the Hambleden room a very Italianate mood.

A PRETTY PAINTED LATE eighteenth-century chair with its original decoration complements the blue and white colour scheme in the attic bedroom.

RIGHT: AN ATTIC GUEST bedroom at Hambleden. With its delicate all-over pattern, this room reflects Fowler's love of France.

THE MAHOGANY CHEST OF drawers was painted to complete the room's scheme.

spirit of nineteenth-century Italy about the room, perhaps something to do with the openness of the planning, as if the expected day-time heat could only be tolerated by such a feeling of airiness. The room's contents contribute to this Italianate mood: the chandelier that Fowler designed and had made in Venice, the painted Continental over-door and Claude Lorraine's Classical capriccio of St Paul landing in Italy over the chimney-piece all play their part. Even the English pieces seem to have absorbed the atmosphere: Chippendale's carved and gilded rococo picture frame, a masterpiece of naval trophies and a pair of English console tables more reminiscent of the Turin cabinet-maker Piffetti's designs than anything from our islands. The little views of Naples and Rome, like mementoes from a Victorian grand tour, are tied to a guilloche braid and tell the same story. The draped cloth over the piano and the deep-buttoned ottoman in green velour, on the other hand, have an Edwardian feel. As a result the room does not appear to have been set in any one period, but to have changed over the decades through continuous use and adaption.

In a small guest bedroom in the attic the mood is distinctly French. It reflects Fowler's love of sophisticated French decoration of a provincial sort, and particularly the practice of using an all-over pattern throughout a room. The little floral patterned *toile*, blue on a white ground, has been used on the walls, ceiling, corner tester, curtains and the chair squab. Set against a white carpet and white furniture, it all suggests a delicate femininity, a modesty hinting at innocence. The two or three touches of colour that depart from the main theme – the lavender blue on the lampshade and the apple green lining to the tester curtains – are delightful.

51

Another client whose ideas were very much in sympathy with Fowler's was Mrs David Bruce, the wife of the American Ambassador. Nancy Lancaster was a close friend and had taken Fowler to meet the Bruces at their official residence, La Pavilion de la Lanterne, while he was working for the Duke and Duchess of Windsor outside Paris. Some years later, the Bruces acquired an apartment in London consisting of a series of rooms of great architectural promise.

The whole concept of this apartment is modelled on a Louis XVI Parisian prototype. A formal hall, leading off a severe communal stone staircase, has a pair of doors, painted drab, under an original fanlight, Directoire in design. On either side of the entrance, bookcases behind open mesh grills and French side chairs are an introduction to the architectural sophistication of the whole apartment. The two reception rooms, connected by double doors on their central axis, are small in size but grand in scale and sublimely elegant. The sitting room with its Ionic order framing the chimney-piece at one end

MRS EVANGELINE BRUCE'S drawing room with the dining room beyond. This apartment was originally modelled on a Louis XVI Parisian prototype and its predominantly French furniture reinforces this spirit.

52

balanced by a high elaborately carved door-case at the other, suggests a stage for some elegant nineteenth-century soirée. The diminutive panelled dining room with its huge niche, large-scaled window and chimney-piece has a verticality that is positively noble. The choice of grey-white paintwork, and an Empire chandelier and chairs, underline the very Frenchness of the place.

The drawing room is painted an Italianate yellow, warmer and softer than Fowler often used in his work, and has a dry finish. The dado, pilasters, chimney-piece and entablature are all in soft whites. Against this back-drop the blues of the picture sashes, cushions and upholstery positively sparkle. The Aubusson carpet, with its brown border, throws into relief the pale ground and all the fresh colours of the centre medallion, bows and garlands. The painted cushions of pomegranates on silk are by the hand of George Oakes. The furniture, a mixture of Louis XVI *bergères* and an English armchair in the French taste, have a refined delicacy of line that suits the architectural mood to

A DETAIL OF THE CURTAINS' double flounces. From time to time the scalloped edges are trimmed with nail scissors.

RIGHT: A CORNER OF MRS Bruce's drawing room. The hand painted silk cushion is by George Oakes.

ABOVE: A DELIGHTFUL WAY TO tie two dissimilar elements together visually. The secret is never to overdo a good idea, otherwise it becomes devalued.

OVERLEAF: MRS BRUCE'S DINING room, which is extraordinarily high for its size, underlines the truth that height, not length or breadth, determines scale.

perfection. The composition of pictures, brackets and pots give emphasis to the room's height, which is its most dramatic feature. The curtains are a *tour-de-force*. Inspired by an eighteenth-century costume design, they are made in oyster silk *faille*. The over-draperies with their elaborate swags and tails are trimmed with double ruffles, scalloped and pinked, with a pair of bows and a centre *chou* catching the draperies at the head. The draw curtains are of apricot silk and there are window seats to match. This room has been planned so that it can seat twelve, or even more at a pinch – ideal for an owner who spends only part of the year in London and who has many friends to entertain.

A CORNER OF PAULINE DE Rothschild's sitting room in the Albany. The curtains are made of unlined pure silk taffeta cut out with pinking shears.

In an Albany apartment, or set as it is rather idiosyncratically known, Fowler found himself working for a client with very individual ideas about lifestyle. Pauline de Rothschild had a panache that was irresistible and together they produced an extraordinary apartment which is both rich and minimalist, formal and free-form, qualities that are normally contradictory. This grand London drawing room has, in effect, been conceived as a studio, but one that has been finished with the most elaborate painted effects. The Ionic pilasters, dado, skirting and floor are all variously painted to simulate marble. The walls are stippled in a putty colour so that the turquoise blue of the pilasters and the entablature's frieze appear to glow. The lightest of the off-whites used on much of the architectural detail is muted so that the oyster silk on the upholstery and curtains looks quite pale. This is the most subtle scheme because the room appears to be much lighter than it is and therefore has a tranquillity that an aggressive white could never achieve.

The highly theatrical silk taffeta curtains, with a complement of bows, were based on a French eighteenth-century drawing; their raw edges, cut with pinking shears, hang one metre on to the floor. These curtains were actually constructed three times over. First they were made in cotton to work out the design. While the curtain maker was half way through the second cutting he was seen to hesitate. 'Don't hesitate,' Fowler told him, 'you've lost the rhythm and you will never get the cut right.' He was therefore made to start all over again.

The sofa bed in a silk check and the Louis XVI suite in blue and ivory were both conceived so as to provide huge scale. The rest of the furniture is an eclectic mixture of eighteenth-century 'Chinese export', *retour d'Egypte* chairs and a *Régence* mirror as well as two or three modern imitation tortoise-shell perspex occasional tables. All this diversity of design, together with the amorphous forms of the fur rugs which appear to float free on the pale painted floor, has been conceived in a free-form manner that is more akin to abstract art than any traditional precepts. A drawing is propped asymetrically on the mantle, along with a few other objects. In the bedroom, a canopied bed, exquisitely detailed, stands as a single object in an almost empty space. The very looseness and freedom of the planning throughout these rooms suggest an energetic spirit always on the move.

THE CURTAINS IN THE ALBANY sitting room, with bows running down their sides, drop one metre on to the floor.

LEFT: THE CANOPIED BED IN the master bedroom stands as a single exquisite object in an almost empty space.

UPPARK, SUSSEX, WAS A HOUSE for which Fowler had great affection.

AT SUDBURY HALL, Derbyshire, Fowler painted Edward Pierce's staircase white – 'a very bold decision', as the Duchess of Devonshire pointed out.

The interiors illustrated in this section of the book only touch on a fraction of John Fowler's work and ideas. These houses, and some of them were very large, involved a huge amount of detail and the work was often spread over many years; Grimsthorpe Castle, for instance, took five. The thread that runs through them all, however, is the sympathy that he had for both clients and architecture, and the influence he still has on our work today. What is more difficult to convey is the trouble he took to accommodate his clients to enable them to 'make do' by re-using old curtains and correcting their mistakes when they had 'had a go' themselves. Lady Hambleden remembers having bought some fabric without being sure whether she liked it, let alone knowing what to do with it. However, he was happy to accept her choice and, with the addition of one or two fabrics of his own choosing, a charming room was created. In another instance, she felt the red Fowler had used on the walls of her sitting room was inappropriate. He immediately conceded the point and so it was changed, along with everything else in the room. At the same time he was prepared to teach local painters a special technique and to use his client's own 'little women' in the village to make slip-covers or to do minor upholstery.

John Fowler's association with the National Trust began in 1956. It came about through his long friendship with James Lees-Milne who a few years earlier had handed over the secretaryship of the Trust's Historic Buildings to Robin Fedden. The arrangement began as an informal one, although later it was to occupy a great deal of his time. After he retired from the company in 1969, due to poor health, he devoted his remaining years to the restoration and refurbishment of over twenty-five houses for the Trust. The Duchess of Devonshire, with whom he enjoyed a particularly good relationship while serving on the same committee for the restoration of Sudbury Hall in Derbyshire, provides an amusing insight into his manner at this period of his life. He was immensely energetic and as determined as 'a terrier after a rat' when it came to detail. 'John made decisions. Sometimes he did not even tell us what he had in mind; we just arrived and found it done. Painting the staircase white, for instance: a very bold decision.' At the time, he was severely criticized for his painting of this important Edward Pierce staircase, but since then it has been established, from records to which he had no access, that this was historically correct.

It should be remembered that the whole approach to the restoration of National Trust houses was then far less academic than it is today. Historical documents were rarely made available and when they were, as at Clandon Park in Surrey, he would spend days pouring over them. There were also considerable financial restraints, so that great ingenuity and a fine sense of priority was needed to achieve the best results. At Uppark, the house for which he had the most affection, he advised the Trust to simply wash the walls down and retouch rather than repaint. In other houses he confined himself simply to rearranging the furniture, editing out what was inappropriate or regrouping and rehanging pictures. His aim was to make sense of these rooms by coaxing them into life so that the public could appreciate how they had once been used. Tom Parr has summed up Fowler's

contribution to the National Trust thus: 'What does it matter if John Fowler shifted the goal posts a little in total historical accuracy? What he has done is to capture the feeling of a room in the period to which it is restored. He has brought back warmth and attractiveness to disused rooms, so reviving an interest in the houses themselves.'

In spite of serious illness, John Fowler worked on gallantly for his remaining years. He is remembered as being quite matter-of-fact about cancer and approaching death, discussing the matter at lunch one day as briskly as if he were referring to his garden and the dying back of plants in autumn. On 27th October 1977 John Fowler died in his sleep at the place he loved best of all, the Hunting Lodge at Odiham in Hampshire.

From the late 1940s, when he acquired it, up until his death, the Hunting Lodge was the pivot of John Fowler's social and creative life. At weekends it was constantly full of friends, many of them clients, and here he was transformed, sharing his inspiration and enthusiasms. The house had been built in the middle of the eighteenth century as a folly, an eyecatcher to be viewed from Dogmersfield Park, which stood a little over a mile away. It had the sort of colourful history that Fowler loved. King John was supposed to have used a *rendezvous de chasse* that had previously stood on the site and, as a young prince, Henry VIII is believed to have met Catharine of Aragon here on her progress to London for her betrothal to his elder brother Prince Arthur.

AT CLANDON PARK, SURREY, Fowler did his finest work for the National Trust. In the Saloon he restored the ceiling to its original colours and painted the overmantle to match the chimney-piece. It now has a proper architectural logic which it never had when it was white.

ONE OF A PAIR OF RUSTIC stone statues on the south front of the Hunting Lodge, John Fowler's country home at Odiham, Hampshire.

BELOW: ONE OF A PAIR OF summer houses that Fowler built on a subordinate axis to the main prospect from the house.

THE HUNTING LODGE'S MAIN elevation, originally painted white, had been designed in the eighteenth century as an eyecatching folly to be viewed from Dogmersfield Park. The pleached hornbeams were planted by Fowler as soon as he bought the property.

In the manner of all the best follies, this building has a presence quite disproportionate to its size. It has a high, rosy pink brick façade consisting of three tall curvilinear Gothic gables surmounted by finials, the central section being dominant. There are Gothic windows on the ground and first floor and blind windows in the gables to an imaginary second floor completing the composition. A small cottage had been built behind this façade with an odd arrangement of rooms that only a talent such as Fowler's could make perfect.

The house and garden are totally integrated in their design, the one fundamental to the other, an expression of complete harmony. The garden combines French formality with that romantic English taste that borders on a glorious untidiness. Its basic structure is the central axis between the house and the lake to the south. He planted two lines of hornbeams, pleached and shaped to frame the lake with its island in the middle. Looking back, the façade of the house becomes a backdrop, a stage awaiting the fantasies of Miss Moberley's imagination. The influence of Marie Antoinette's Hameau, that balance between sophistication and charmed simplicity, pervades the spirit of the place. There are a pair of Gothic summer houses on a subordinate axis at right angles to the main prospect, but this is only one of the many small surprises to be discovered on walks through these gardens.

Barbara Oakley, a landscape gardener and a cousin of Fowler's, wrote a description of his gardening skills that could easily stand for his talents as a decorator:

John's gardening was a metaphysical part of his whole personality. It exemplified his passionate belief in perfection without pedantry, romanticism without sloppiness and an unfailing

instinct for quality whether perceived in the sparkle of a celandine or the elegance of a rose. A cluster of snowdrops showing though half-melted snow probably gave him as much pleasure as summer's pink geraniums spiked unexpectantly with scarlet, tumbling from elegant tubs on Gothic stands placed symmetrically on the brick terrace by the house.
Who else could have used such dashingly unexpected plantings, cottage charm, and elegant formality on the grand scale as he did? His gardening was as subtle and surprising as his interior design.'

John Fowler was a born teacher; he took great interest in discussing ideas and contributing the knowledge he had acquired over the years. There would always be one such session in any weekend, sometimes late into the night after supper or on visiting whatever house he might be working on. It was this pleasure in sharing that was reflected in the conception of the folly and made it such a memorable and influential place. 'The Hunting Lodge was the acme of simplicity, but not in the least cottagey. It had supreme elegance, but was not in the least over-grand,' his friend Stephen Long, the antique dealer, once observed. Of even greater significance was the spirit he breathed into the place. Everything was for the benefit of his friends. His own bedroom was small and plain; the principal guest bedroom was a delight. The food, flowers, wine and entertainments were all planned with the utmost care and forethought, but the hospitality was nevertheless spontaneously given.

ABOVE AND BELOW: THE dining hall at the Hunting Lodge was furnished as an anteroom. Comfortable chairs and a pretty painted commode, an *étagère*, delightful pictures and prints give it a lived-in appeal as Fowler hated the baleful look of an unused dining room.

The decoration of the Hunting Lodge was a focus of all his experiences and passions in life. Like someone who remains constant to his former friends, however much his own circumstances have improved, he honoured his earliest love of simplicity. Both the garden and the house owed their origins to the 'humble elegance' of the top floor at 292 King's Road and the cottage at Maytham. To this he added a veneer of sophistication, combined with an informality that he thought essential for comfort. The garden did not change; in fact, he told Stephen Long that he never altered a single line of his first sketch for it. The house only changed a little, with subtle improvements to the fabrics and with better furniture.

As the approach to the house is from the back, the visitor's first sight is of the untidy form of the end gables and walls covered in a garland rose, climbing hydrangeas and camellias. There is no hint of the ordered Gothic splendour on the other side, nor the architectural form of the garden. It is only the later addition of a small clapboard entrance hall and a Georgian front door flanked by two *tôle* wall lanterns that suggest the internal discipline. Inside, the hall is tiny, its decoration Classical with French overtones. It has a dry scrubbed chestnut floor and walls in tones of biscuit with soft white woodwork. A *demi-lune* console table with a marble top painted in off-whites faces the entrance, with the marble relief of Caesar from 292 above it. A pair of eighteenth-century painted Gothic chairs and English prints on the walls also reflect this exercise in miniature of all that he loved in English and French decoration.

BELOW: THE HUNTING LODGE'S tiny entrance hall has a mixture of English and French decoration. The Gothic Revival chair is one of a pair that stood either side of the door.

RIGHT: THE ENTRANCE HALL, with a *demi-lune* console table painted in off-whites and above it the marble relief of Caesar from 292 King's Road. The pretty Aubusson rug softens the formality of the decoration.

The main purpose of the addition was to remove the entrance from the original hall, which then could be used as a dining room. The space was long and narrow, but Fowler managed to turn its difficult proportions to advantage. Because he disliked the bleak inflexibility of a dining room, particularly in these circumstances where one had to pass through it all the time, it was furnished as an anteroom. There are comfortable chairs either side of a simple Georgian fireplace and an Italian painted commode with a pretty running design of tiny green leaves on a cream ground. Early seventeenth-century Besler botanical prints, Chinese glass pictures and a Regency *étagère* produce the necessary informality.

The simple round Regency dining table is pushed up into the corner overlooking the garden and around the table are six Dutch painted chairs with original, much-worn neo-Classical decoration, in *grisaille* on a brown ground. Diminutive Versailles tubs and *cache-pots* of painted tin contained delightful plants such as mophead box and amaryllis. His table was given great attention and in spring a *tôle* vase candelabrum with tulip candle-holders would be filled with real flowers. With his preference for the modest, he chose country plates and thick nineteenth-century moulded French wine glasses. This room has an original, very worn red square-tiled floor and the uneven plaster walls are painted to simulate panelling. He devised a pale stone-coloured ground with a French lilac grey for the stiles and rails; shadows and highlights were then painted to complete the illusion.

For the curtains to the one original Gothic lancet window in this room, a red-brown strawberry leaf pattern is used, the trefoil leaf form creating just the right medieval mood. The pelmet is shaped to reflect the window-head. The other two windows in the room are more recent additions of conventional design and the curtains in yellow diamond cloth are treated simply with French headings.

The sitting room, which centres on the front elevation, is small but never feels so. The furniture is all arranged around the Georgian fireplace opposite the garden door which is flanked by two more lancet windows. All three openings have simple curtains hanging from iron rods. The off-white fabric has a hand-block-printed running pattern of alternate diamond shapes and quatrefoils that look appropriately Gothic. The rough plaster walls are washed in a sienna pink that lifts the spirits. The carpet is the same 'mouseback' beige as was used at Haseley and runs through all the upstairs rooms.

In the sitting room formality is only hinted at by a beautiful serpentine-fronted commode with its central medallion and swagged husk decoration; above it hangs a portrait of an Irish forebear. The brown rope from which the picture is suspended and the pair of bell pulls produce a structured composition, a vignette of something altogether grander. While the sharp yellow of the sofa and easy chair cools the colour scheme, the pretty painted blind-fret table in a sharper vermilion and white adds spice. The deep green of the fringed velour 'Friar's' chair corresponds to the deep green leaves always in the room and a lift is given by one of the prettiest of the Colefax chintzes 'Old Rose with Fancy'. The simple elegance of the English painted

THE HUNTING LODGE SITTING room has rough plaster walls that have been washed in a sienna pink. The deep green of the fringed velour Friar's chair acts as a counterpoint to the pinks in the chintz and the vermilion of the blind-fret occasional table.

HERE FOWLER HAS CREATED A formal composition with the pair of bell pulls, the candlesticks and a portrait of an Irish forebear.

OPPOSITE: IN THE TINY SITTING room the sofa, comfortable chairs and stool are all arranged around the fireplace for Fowler's weekend entertaining.

Marie Antoinette's gloves in a frame hanging on the wall half way up.

LEFT: FOWLER'S TINY bookroom study is dominated by the huge pattern of the Mauny wallpaper 'Primavères'. It helped to overcome the awkward presence of the staircase, which took up the whole of the back wall.

armchair in the French taste relieves the comfortable lumpishness of the upholstery.

John Fowler's study was beyond the sitting room, a tiny book-room with the staircase taking up the whole of the back wall. A French *secrétaire*, simple bookstacks and one desk chair was all that could be fitted into the space. The geometry of the room was there-fore untidy and Fowler's solution was very clever. He used the huge scale of the Mauny wallpaper 'Primavères', in warm yellow-brown tones, to smother the problem. The huge serpentine pattern, with its bold blooms, is all that one notices. The awkward cramped stairs and bookshelves look passive in this context.

The principal bedroom above the sitting room has a pronounced romantic French mood, with an English accent. This is created by the floral stripes on the walls and the English chintz on the tester. The ver-tical stripes have been made from a Mauny wallpaper border inge-niously pasted on to the pale cerulean blue distemper walls. There is a poignancy about this sophisticated idea seen in such rustic circumstances. The simple boarded doors, the rough walls and the 'mouse-back'-coloured carpet have the appeal of a pretty servant girl from a William Ward print. The simple white curtains are bound in red; the pelmets again have been shaped to match the heads of the lancet windows behind them. A pair of Italian painted chairs, an English patchwork bed quilt and the modest pictures all contribute to the freshness of the room's decoration.

John Fowler's painted fresco decoration on the inside of one of the two garden pavilions shows the depth of his romantic spirit. The vigour that has been given to the freely-painted sienna ground is both deliberate and subtle; the cool of the *grisaille*, which he used to paint the young oaks and to give the deep brown shadows extra weight, is masterly. This wall demonstrates that his gifts as a decorative painter rose above the ordinary. The stylized expression that he gave to his technique belongs to the eighteenth-century Classical tradition. It is no pastiche, however, for he felt that a closeness to nature was of fundamental importance to us all. This was the common bond that enabled Nancy Lancaster and John Fowler to work so well together. They both appreciated that decoration is only a background to life, a discipline through which one can be generous and from which memorable moments are created and lasting friendships forged.

JOHN'S *GRISAILLE* PAINTING OF young oaks on a sienna ground is masterly and shows the depth of his romantic spirit.

THE USE OF THE MAUNY wallpaper border between the principal guest bedroom windows ingeniously ties the oval pictures to the wall decoration.

RIGHT: THE CHINTZ OF THE BED drapes delightfully matches the paper border in the principal guest bedroom.

PART II
HALLMARKS OF
COLEFAX & FOWLER'S STYLE

'I'M AGIN DECORATION; I'M JUST A PERCOLATOR OF IDEAS,' NANCY LANCASTER ONCE remarked. It might appear idiotic that such a statement could be interpreted to represent the philosophy of a firm such as Colefax & Fowler. However, in its proper context, this observation makes some sense.

Our obligation in decorating houses covers a wide range of considerations. But at the core of it all is the supreme aim of creating comfort so that people can find peace and harmony in an increasingly unsettled world. Rural life and nature have, as a consequence, been important sources of inspiration. In England, there exists a long tradition of turning to the country because of a deep-seated love for the way of life it affords. Country houses have been touched by many changes, but often seem to have benefited, possessing certain qualities of them all: a patchwork of ideas and pastimes. The English country house style therefore appears to be an evolutionary process rather than an active expression of any artistic ideals.

The essence of this style is the layering of succeeding ideologies, mixed up with what is usually found in the houses themselves, such as neglect, custom and attachment. It achieves an atmosphere that has apparently emerged as a result of osmosis rather than of any planned creative process. It is nostalgic, an ingredient that has been deeply embedded in our art and architecture for the last 400 years. In fact, what appears to be an appealing disorder is an illusion: the ideas behind decoration are thought out most carefully. Nancy's statement is therefore about the ultimate objective, or how things should appear when complete, and not about the means to fulfilling that end. What she is really proposing is that houses should look well used, well loved and elegant, so that friends and guests can be put at their ease by the unaffectedness of their surroundings.

This is an approach to decoration in which intuition plays an important part. Although it can be the dissimilarities between objects or furniture that establish the character of the room, there must always be a relationship of some sort between the things used. This need not be academic or historical; it might be visual, to do with colour, mood, scale or pattern. In this way a room becomes a means of personal expression, which gives it life. Whereas the best of such rooms appear charming, witty and informal, the basis of their composition is serious. All the elements must be considered and designed with great thoroughness. The following chapters discuss the way in which Colefax & Fowler approaches such issues.

The Conception of a Room

Up UNTIL THIS CENTURY THE APPROACH TO THE PLANNING AND decoration of notable houses was formal. Comfort and convenience did not play the essential role that they do today since there was an army of staff to fetch, carry and set things straight. Taste was important and, as a gentleman's home was the centre of his life and the means by which his social standing was proclaimed, great efforts were made to create gardens, architecture and interiors that reflected his status. The creativity that went into such artifices as the heavenly rococo dream of the Hall at Harlaxton Manor in Lincolnshire, the Chinese Bedroom at Claydon House, Buckinghamshire, or the overwhelming exoticism of the Royal Pavilion, Brighton, might appear frivolous; but the motives behind such ingenuity and expense were serious. To be recognized as being erudite and a man of fashion was a boost to a person's rank in an already exclusive world: it was a brewer, for example, who committed himself to building the neo-Palladian masterpiece Southill, in Bedfordshire, and there were others in trade who did much the same.

Today, the motives that people have for decorating their homes remain largely unchanged. It is a means of personal expression and a source of pride, especially at a time when any ostentatious display in public is considered bad taste. However, the approach to designing and decorating houses now begins differently; everything starts with an analysis of living patterns of a detail that would have amazed our forebears. Whereas they built the great houses for perpetuity, we design only for a portion of one individual lifespan. Personal requirements therefore have become the main focus of our attention. The spaces that we have to deal with tend to be smaller and fewer in number than in the past. Small rooms involve making imaginative use of the available space, and even larger ones call for all sorts of exercises in flexibility.

Our attitudes to furniture and its organization have also changed. Where once such items were regarded as being subservient to an overall vision, now they are subject to more pragmatic considerations. What takes priority is the way in which people can most comfortably sit together and most conveniently use the furniture. John Fowler's answer to an inquiry about his basic concept for the decoration of the Hunting Lodge was, surprisingly, 'To feel that one can sit down anywhere without having to move a chair'. This observation, which could only have been made in our time, clearly reflects his priorities of comfort and convenience.

TOP: A VARIETY OF FURNITURE to suit adults and children alike, with the prerequisite round table for games, 'prep' or a television supper.

ABOVE: ALL THE EQUIPMENT can be hidden away.

RIGHT: TWO SMALL FRENCH *bergères* either side of the fireplace face into the body of the room.

THE VIZAGAPATNAM CHAIRS (on the right) are a good example of the kind of eccentric pieces that are now enthusiastically sought. The composition of the overmantle is reflected in the recessed shelves either side.

When he was dividing his life between his lodge in Hampshire and 292 King's Road, Fowler was faced with the problem of planning both establishments so that he could entertain, and live stylishly, in rooms that had been conceived for a meaner way of life. His solution lay partly in mixing the grand with the modest, the shabby with the elegant, and in injecting charming colours and pretty fabrics. Even more important were the principles that governed the organization of the furniture. These, which Fowler arrived at largely through trial and error and can best be seen at the Hunting Lodge, became the basis of his planning in all the houses that he subsequently decorated.

Ever since, all of us at Colefax & Fowler have been using these principles, which are a matter of organizing as much seating as possible into any given space so that it looks informal without being arbitrary. For example, two single chairs placed by the fire facing towards the body of the room, although they may be hard and small, are often the first to be occupied. As the fire is a focus of attention, no occupant feels hard done by sitting next to it. An upholstered stool or ottoman, sometimes trefoil or round in shape but more usually rectangular, is essential. When the room is packed one or two people can sit on it; otherwise it is a useful surface for magazines, a tea tray or one's feet. An upholstered fender or 'bum rack' is extremely practical; it does not clutter up a small room when not in use and yet can take up to three people when the occasion demands. The dreadful three-piece suite of

IN THE COUNTRY SITTING ROOM photographed on these two pages a perfect balance of luxury and informality has been established. The plumpness of the French *bergère* and the stool is typical of the domed form of French upholstery.

THIS DECALCOMANIA LAMP, with its gathered cream silk shade and frill has a softness of form that suits this country setting.

the interwar years, which amazingly still lingers on, has no place in this scheme of things. The upholstery that we look for, like the case furniture and tables, should offer variety in size and purpose. The idea is to produce a plan that strikes a balance between the natural patterns of sitting around a chosen focal point, such as a fireplace or a bay window, and a slightly untidy disposition of things that suggests a lifestyle enjoyed spontaneously.

The freedom with which various types of furniture are mixed together derives its inspiration from large country houses as they have

ABOVE AND BELOW: THIS garden hall captures the country mood. The Regency flower table and the Besler prints (they once belonged to John Fowler) serve the ever-changing arrangement of plants to perfection.

mellowed and become comfortable over the generations. It is comfort in its many forms that lies behind all our pursuits. The comfort of sitting, with an adjacent table at the correct height, a lamp on it casting a perfect light on to your book and not into your eyes; the comfort, albeit visual, of objects balanced and arranged on tables and on walls. It should be remembered that the spaces between things are as important as the elements themselves. If the planning of furniture, for whatever reason, is packed and dense, then this should be echoed throughout the decoration to keep the balance. The distribution of elements should relate to the basic design idea. A room might be neo-Classical in concept, with the structured discipline of a Charles Percier interior, as is hinted at in David's painting of Madame Recamier, or have the compressed overall patterning of a Vuillard domestic scene. It is inappropriate that the two approaches should be mixed, for each has its own characteristic form and style.

Chairs and sofas, some large and others small, should be so arranged that they 'talk' to one another; that is, they should be conveniently placed so that three or four people can form a conversation group. As it is preferable that a group should not get too large, a second or, in larger rooms, a third is formed. It is much more satisfactory to have two or three separate pockets of conversation than a single, large group dominated by one or two people.

When choosing tables, a variety in design looks best, although they must be at a sensible height in relation to any adjacent seating. Conventional tables tend to be skeletal structures and a surfeit of legs gives a rather thin and cluttered appearance to a room. We therefore look for alternative pieces to compensate for this; they are usually those that have some mass, such as black lacquer tea chests, upholstered ottomans and antique work tables of the kind that were used by ladies in which to keep their embroidery silks, wool, beads and bobbins. Many years ago, John Fowler found one of the most ingenious pieces: a small free-standing Regency cupboard with a table top on four telescopic legs that could be adjusted to any required height. Hybrid pieces such as these are much sought after by all the Colefax & Fowler decorators because they are generally odd and often witty.

Mass can also be achieved by skirted tables and colours can be used on them in a way that picks up others in the room. The tables can be round or octagonal, but the cloths hang best when they are lined and have a heavy wool bullion fringe around the base; the skirt should break on the floor. Antique felt appliqué cloths or even patchwork quilts can be adapted for this purpose. The addition of this sort of worked and complicated pattern can introduce a charming spirit into a room, especially if the other fabrics are quite formal.

Rooms always benefit from a change of scale, and large pieces of furniture provide this as well as establishing a valuable link between the architecture and the room's decoration. This is why libraries with floor-to-ceiling bookcases can be so dramatic. In sitting rooms, drawing rooms and studies, the use of high bookcases, built-in shelves, chests on stands, Chinese coromandel lacquer screens or even a massive picture with a frame to match will all achieve this effect. In dining rooms, tall pieces of furniture are generally uncalled for, so height should be established through collections of prints, plates, pictures or other wall decorations. As attention is so centrally focused on the table and chairs, a large chandelier or antique colza oil light hanging from above can provide this balance within the room. In bedrooms, four-poster and half-tester beds and wardrobes do the same.

LIGHT OPEN ARMCHAIRS, besides looking pretty, can be moved around so conveniently – hence their French name *chaises volantes*.

THIS LARGE, LOW SITTING room in the Scottish Highlands has a number of seating groups. The side table and the pair of lamps help to define the spaces they occupy.

Variety in scale and composition is particularly important in relation to walls. Drawings by architects such as Robert Adam and John Papworth illustrate their considerable interest in handling such decorative elements within their architecture. There is also the example of Sir John Soane's own house in Lincoln's Inn Fields which is simply crammed with antiquities, plaster casts, drawings and paintings, of a density that must have been rare even amongst the most obsessional collectors of the time. By the middle of the nineteenth century, the principles of this approach were so well understood that just about anything that could be hung on walls by way of decoration was: armour, flags, guns, spears, stags' antlers, trophies, china antiquities, prints and, of course, pictures. Today our objective is to create compositions of an architectural nature, with a preference for a vertical emphasis, as this corresponds to the rules that lie behind all Classical building.

The strongest elements to be used should be placed either at the top, or at least above the centre of any grouping in much the same way as the pedimented overdoors or the elaborate crestings to mirrors relate to what is below them. There is also a practical reason for this: small intimate drawings and miniatures should be set approximately at eye level where they can be seen in comfort from a sitting position. Large-scale decorations or works of art that can be 'stood back from' deserve to go higher. Brackets on which pots or busts can be placed give relief to an otherwise flat decorative scheme. This device looks best when there is some intellectual or decorative link between the wall decoration and whatever is supported on the brackets. Busts of emperors, for example, would go ideally with neo-Classical decoration; a pair of Chinese birds could well echo the spirit of a Chinese wallpaper. The same tenets apply to objects, sculptures and china when placed in cabinets or on shelves.

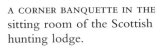

A CORNER BANQUETTE IN THE sitting room of the Scottish hunting lodge.

The tops of side tables are often treated in a similar fashion: the larger objects are placed at the back as this gives presence to any tablescape. It is often more aesthetically satisfactory to work around a symmetrical arrangement, such as pairs of objects – pots, *jardinières*, or sculptures of complementary scale – in a manner that was much favoured by John Fowler. The alternative is to build everything around one dominant piece to which all else is subordinate. Within a room, one would probably adopt both options. Equally, one table might display a collection of things that are of the same scale, colour or origin or that are simply amusing in their relationship to one another.

The one great advantage that we have in this century is electric light; and its disposition is of considerable importance. The Colefax & Fowler view has always been that any form of ceiling spotlight for general purpose use is too dramatic and too staged. It throws all the emphasis on to the objects lit, which then have to be significantly impressive to justify it. For this reason, even picture lights should be used with discrimination; there is nothing more pretentious than an indifferent picture that draws attention to itself. Our view is that the people within the room should come first and that, however beautiful the room's contents, they should be secondary, emerging only on discovery, certainly not shouting for attention like some recalcitrant child.

It is our practice to use table lamps with shades almost to the exclusion of all other types of lighting. The unrivalled quality of this system of lighting is that, with the correctly worked-out arrangement of bulbs within the shade, an ideal balance can be achieved. A lamp, especially if it is large, should throw some light on the ceiling, but

A PLEASING VERTICALITY HAS been created on the end wall of this room by the bracket for the blue and white garniture and the picture cords. Without such treatment the decoration would fail to tie in satisfactorily with the other walls.

THE TINY PATTERN ON THIS tightly gathered beige silk shade contrasts well with the cut-glass base.

THESE CAREFULLY FRAMED prints have been arranged in a tight composition that makes excellent decoration.

HANGING SHELVES PROVIDE relief from prints and drawings in bedrooms and studies.

most of the light should flood the table on which the lamp stands as well as filter through the shade itself. In modest rooms card shades can be used. It is also possible to have a gathered printed cotton, with a small busy pattern, as a shade which obviously has an informal look. Pleated silk shades are grander and more formal. Both silk pleats and perforations in card shades, in a number of different designs, give additional interest to the patterns thrown on illuminated surfaces in a room. Tin shades are appropriate with neo-Classical bases, or alternatively in rooms of the period. These are often painted black or dark green, giving them a visual strength not present in other forms of shade.

The placing of lamps around the room is a matter of common sense. They should be on tables adjacent to the main chairs and sofas, or sometimes fixed as adjustable wall lights to bookcase architraves and at either side of chimney-pieces. Pairs of candlestick lamps go well on side tables. Various other forms of lamps, some with swing arms and some with small circular tables large enough to hold an ashtray, a book and a drink, are also used where appropriate. The corners of a room should have lamps wherever possible, at night this gives emphasis to the architecture of the space, as well as making the room look larger. Without lamps, the corners will be shrouded in shadow and the room will tend to look gloomy and formless.

In conclusion, to put a room together with all its contents takes great thought, determination and discipline. The planning and choice of furniture, pictures, lighting, bits and bobs, flowers and pot-pourri should all look comfortable together. To succeed, so that wherever the eye alights the spirits are lifted, is to prove that the effort has been worthwhile.

THE PAIR OF LOOKING GLASSES above the lamps not only reflect a certain amount of daytime and evening light, but also give depth to this fireplace wall.

CHAPTER 5   # The Application of Paint

SWAGGED BLUE DRAPERY HELD with ties at the head of each swag – all in *trompe l'oeil*. Garlands of *grisaille* flowers frame the cartouche and hang at intervals around the room.

OPPOSITE: THE CIRCULAR closet, Syon House, painted by John Fowler in shades of blue and off-white on a pink ground, with a delicate picking-out in gold leaf.

PAINT, ON WALLS AND ON WOODWORK, MORE THAN ANY OTHER attribute establishes the character of an interior. An empty room that is well painted shows the truth of this. The manner in which the subject is approached reveals absolutely a designer's understanding of decoration and his ability to pull together all that he has to work with. It is a task that demands both imagination and sensitivity. A decorator who has, and uses, this feel for colour, tone and texture sets himself apart from others in his field every bit as much as a great painter stands out from his contemporaries. It is a talent that is instantly recognizable and just as memorable.

John Fowler's approach to paint was that of a romantic, one who loves and breathes the atmosphere of old places. His was a subtle

79

talent that understood the balance between restraint and creativity. Cottages and modest places were washed out in water-based distemper because the dry quality of this medium allowed the colours to speak for themselves so wonderfully. Until this century distemper was always used in cottages and so was the appropriate material; besides, there was a rusticity about it that appealed to his appreciation of the humble. Its dry, matt surface enables the colour to be seen in its pure state. With oil-bound paints the medium itself reflects the light, thereby diluting the purity of the pigment. They are, however, much more durable and resilient. When it came to painting furniture and the woodwork Fowler used either oil paint or oil-bound distemper and watercolour for the decoration, but the touch was always light. The coats of colour were applied thinly and sometimes with the most delicate picking out. This produced an illusive surface that was pleasing to the eye, a visual softness which appeared to absorb the light and to have been faded by it.

Fowler's early experience in restoring and recreating the painted decoration on antique French *fauteuils* and Regency furniture inspired him to work towards that range of painting techniques that the firm still uses today. George Oakes, who first worked with Fowler in 1956 and now runs the Colefax & Fowler decoration and fabric studio which was built on this heritage, remembers that one of his first jobs was the painting of a Chinoiserie wallpaper for Grimsthorpe Castle. The long panels were laid out on trestle tables in the attic room at Brook Street. After this the work involved a variety of things from painting furniture and screens to decorating materials for commissioned tablecloths, cushions and even curtains. The painted borders to the sequinned-spangled curtains and cushions at Daylesford, the late eighteenth-century house in Gloucestershire built for Warren Hastings, were examples of the more exotic work they executed together.

A MELLOW HONEY COLOUR HAS been applied as a glaze to these cottage walls.

THESE CHAIRS ARE COPIES OF AN original eighteenth-century painted chair which had been acquired for a client. The decoration is an imitation of a chintz which probably covered the upholstery.

A RECENT SAMPLEBOARD OF painted decoration from the Colefax & Fowler studio for a tester frame in the Regency manner. The urn and swags in *grisaille* on a yellow ground represent the central motif on the front of the bed.

AT SUDELEY CASTLE, Gloucestershire, the walls' stencil decoration – appropriate in such early architecture – was inspired by a carved Tudor detail found elsewhere in the building.

Since then more artists have joined the firm and now carry out an even more involved body of work: painted rooms, painted floors, *trompes l'oeil*, designs for chintzes and carpets and almost anything else that might need co-ordinating with some specific decorative concept.

How to paint the interiors of fine houses which contain good furniture, carpets and pictures is a much-debated question posing a fundamental dilemma. Should the paintwork be restored to its original state using the colours, the medium and method of application that was originally intended in the eighteenth or nineteenth centuries? Or should the decorator pursue other objectives, freer from such constraints? The difficulty with the former approach, which at present is much in vogue, is that the result appears both startling and completely fresh to our eyes. Antique carpets, needlework, wallpapers and fabrics have faded hugely over the years. Furniture and pictures have darkened so much that we would barely recognize them in their original states. The gilding of console tables, pier glasses and other enrichment has now become dull and patinated and in many cases the original preparation, the red bolus, is all that remains of the highlights. To put antiques of any quality or charm into rooms that have been restored to their authentic colours produces an unhappy result. The furniture is debased because it looks shabby when set against such perfection of finish and chromatic intensity and the tonal values within old paintings are rendered nonsensical.

The recent restoration by Ealing Borough Council of Pitshanger Manor, Sir John Soane's house, highlights the problems of a strictly academic approach to paintwork. The breakfast room, now seen without furniture, pictures or sculpture, has little point other than as an exercise in historical accuracy. To understand how these Regency rooms would have looked on completion, they should be seen and enjoyed fully furnished and lit by candle and by colza oil lamps. The stronger colours and burnished surfaces would then have had the correct tonal relationships to one another, especially when seen against the deep shadows cast by this subdued form of lighting. There would have been rhythm and harmony between the colours of the furnishing fabrics, the pictures and the clothes of the day. In the current restoration no pictures or antique furniture could possibly survive the decoration, and so the complete experience will always be denied us. An exact, historical approach in any age is likely to be lifeless and, paradoxically, artificial; better that it should be confined to exhibitions and museums, for it has nothing to do with bringing a room to life.

A LONDON HALL WITH ONE OF a pair of *trompe l'oeil* bas reliefs, just discernable in the mirror's reflection.

ABOVE: A PATTERN OF cornflowers and a folded ribbon for a hand painted wallpaper.

LEFT: SIMULATED MARBLE *trompe l'oeil* bas relief from the hall above.

THE GARDEN DINING ROOM
at West Green House,
Hampshire. Each panel has
been painted with bunches of
imaginary flowers loosely
based on a French eighteenth-
century room.

A CORNER OF THE PALLADIAN
Room at Haseley Court
showing George Oakes's first
painting of the
Drottninghölm paper. The
flowers were finished with
egg-white to glisten in the
candlelight at night.

John Fowler and, in turn, the firm today have always taken a more pragmatic and interpretative view. We believe that the mood of rooms is all-important and therefore the tonal values decided upon, irrespective of the colours themselves, should relate to the things to be used within the interiors. Sometimes colours are smoked, by adding a little black to them, or faded so that the effect is that the room and all its contents have aged with dignity together. No one element should stand out in the context of the whole. At Haseley, George Oakes' painting of the Chinese wallpaper, based on the original paper from Drottninghölm, took into account the mix of old fabrics and furniture. The ground colour was dirtied and patinated and the leaves were umbered before being finished with egg-white so that they would glitter by candlelight at night. The understanding of comfort goes beyond having just the right chair and attendant table at the right height in the right position; it is also a case of capturing something of the spirit of a place. Everything should look natural and inevitable for real comfort to be enjoyed.

When working in old houses it is a good idea to take paint scrapes from walls and woodwork. The colours thereby revealed give valuable historical clues and provide some idea of the original concepts. Colefax & Fowler's approach has generally been to use this information as a starting point. The colours are not, of course, as they would have looked when they were originally applied. People do not, as a rule, paint over bright, fresh-looking walls and so what these scrapes show are the colours faded by light and changed by wear and tear.

Once these finishes have been discovered, paintboards are prepared by the firm to match. The techniques of application frequently used are those that were first brought back into favour by John Fowler and then developed by him and George Oakes to evoke the softness of old tired paintwork. The paint is put on thinly as glazes over either a ground colour or white. It is then given a coat of flat varnish to protect the vulnerable surface, as well as to leave that 'dry' finish which is essential to the look of old paintwork. These thin glazes are almost impossible to apply evenly and so a merit has been made of this difficulty. The quality of paint is determined by the sort of brush with which it is put on. Stippling brushes, for example, give a speckled effect; 'floggers', because of their very long hairs, allow a straight-grained 'dragged' look; and even old worn-out brushes can manipulate the surface glaze in a way that is useful. There are yet other techniques that can be employed, such as ragging, sponging or applying 'under the brush'; each has its own essential quality and is an expression of the method used.

THIS RUNNING LEAF STENCIL decoration has a larger scale than most paper borders and is therefore particularly appropriate in an architectural context as weighty as Sudeley Castle.

TROMPE L'OEIL PANELLING comprising blue styles and rails with off-white panels. This treatment gives an order to walls and generally helps with the organization of pictures and other decorative elements.

RIGHT: THE *TROMPE L'OEIL* bookcase reflected in a mirror.

BELOW: THE LEFT-HAND SIDE OF the bookcase is real, as are the books. The *trompe l'oeil* painting of the bookcase on the right-hand side hides a jib door. Chicken wire, frequently used on provincial bookcases, here covers the false books.

A DETAIL OF THE PAINTED decoration behind the chicken wire.

In recent years a plethora of books on how to use these paint techniques has come on to the market. They have, however, done more to debase the traditional approach to decoration than to further an appreciation of its subtleties. For a successful finish it is necessary to have experience in handling colour, in using the medium confidently and in balancing the tones; apparently this cannot be conveyed by books. The impression has been given that all these methods of painting can be used as an end in themselves, but this is misleading. When applied to architecture, the various techniques should be employed to establish a mood, language, of the architectural components themselves, but the method should barely be noticed. When sensitively applied, paint can suggest a surface that has become thin with age or has been washed too enthusiastically by over-diligent housemaids. Glazes can be applied thinly to give depth and richness, but certainly they should never be part of a bravura exercise.

85

LEFT A *TROMPE L'OEIL* chimney-board of three pots (for use in summer) in George Oakes's own home.

A PAINTED CHEST AS IT WAS supposed to have looked. The fashion for stripping pine has resulted in the loss of much excellent painted decoration.

THE CHIMNEY-BREAST IS painted in imitation of stonework with blocks and mouldings.

When painting country furniture, however, the treatment can be different. Simple pine pieces, mantles and cupboards were often painted boldly to compensate for their very basic design and construction. The crafts of stencilling, as well as combing and sponging paint, were used in the most vigorous manner; the bolder the effect, the better. When we come to decorating rustic buildings or country chests of drawers we often employ such techniques. The fashion for stripping pine, which has been with us for the last twenty or thirty years, is quite incorrect because pine and beech furniture was always painted. We find ourselves using these painting techniques on furniture in order that it can be restored to the way it was intended.

Another type of painting that has been refined by the Colefax & Fowler studio stems from simulated effects. This is a painting technique devised to represent materials such as marble, stone, tortoiseshell, exotic woods and even patterned chintz. The tradition was in vogue throughout Europe in the eighteenth and the first quarter of the nineteenth centuries before its popularity declined. It has a special quality all of its own: it does not look exactly as the original material, but has a painterly character and relates well to many of the fabrics and papers that the firm has developed over the years. It is used on the more important architectural elements of interiors, such as skirting boards, dados, cornices and columns, as well as on floors and walls.

Walls are often painted to simulate panelling; the stiles and rails should be painted considerably darker than the panels, with shadows and highlights being added to give emphasis. These should look as if they have been cast by any available window light so that a three-dimensional effect is created. We have also produced more complicated schemes in which elaborate detail has been added to Gothic-style panelling, and simulated stonework has been painted in with blocks and keystones. Whatever the design, it should be in sympathy with the architecture for the results to add authority to the room. The greatest value in treating walls in this way is that an intermediate scale is introduced, one that lies half way between that of the architecture

EXAMPLES OF GEORGE OAKES'S painted decoration.

A PICTURE AND FRAME PAINTED by George Oakes.

CUSHIONS WITH FLOWERS handpainted on silk. The silk used is a greyed oyster colour, with a dry finish and no slub. This old, irreplaceable silk, inherited from John Fowler, is now virtually finished.

87

and that of the room's contents. More importantly, walls can be effectively 'broken up' into a series of vertical components, thereby overcoming any existing horizontal emphasis. It should be remembered that eighteenth-century taste avoided horizontal compositions in architecture and in interiors, something that one is apt to forget in this post-Bauhaus era.

On furniture, these painting techniques are generally applied to small tables and chests. When a piece is newly made, it can be patinated to produce an impression of considerable age, thus enabling it to be used with antiques. A word of caution: simulated pieces are always inferior to antique painted furniture. They should be kept to a minimum in any one room and confined to practical uses such as bedside and occasional tables.

Another interesting technique that has become a Colefax & Fowler hallmark is the realistic representation of certain forms inspired by eighteenth- and early nineteenth-century chintzes, china and the best antique painted furniture. This decorative painting borders on fine art, as the skills and knowledge necessary to carry it out well are of a very high order. Although John Fowler initially taught George Oakes, it is the latter who has taken this to a level of refinement where he has few equals. The examples of his painted flowers, birds, insects, running designs of leaves and flowers are endless and can be seen on furniture, silk cushions and curtain pelmets. His work also includes screens and murals, some quite simply decorative such as the charming fresco of hops in an old Kent rectory. For hundreds of years the hops that go into the making of English beer have been grown in Kent and this mural is a celebration of the crop in the fields outside, with poppies growing in abundance. The poppies add a dash of colour to this scheme.

TROMPE L'OEIL PANELLING HAS been created here with the aid of Mauny paper mouldings for a richer effect. The skirting has been marblized.

A MURAL DECORATION OF HOPS on climbing frames with occasional poppies adding a dash of red to the scheme.

A SET OF PAINTED OVAL cushions on an eighteenth-century seat.

88

GEORGE OAKES'S MURAL
decoration in the dining room
at Sezincote, Gloucestershire.
This house, one of the most
ambitious to be erected in
Regency England, was built
in the Indian manner and on a
comparable scale with
Brighton Pavilion. These
capriccios, inspired by the
work of the eighteenth-
century English painter
Thomas Daniels, pay their
respects to this Indian
heritage.

THE CHIMNEY-BREAST IS
painted with *trompe l'oeil*
designs of Indian architectural
detail. The dado has been
painted to simulate marble.

The technique of mural painting may take many forms: *trompe l'oeil* pots and plates with all their shadows and highlights; panels in *grisaille*, a technique of painting in greys usually to resemble stone-carved bas-reliefs; and Arcadian scenes which give the illusion of distant perspectives. On a smaller scale, flowers are painted on to silk bell pulls, running garlands are applied to the cornices of four-poster beds and sets of decorative paintings are produced that would be the envy of Samuel Dixon.

The merit of all these painterly techniques is that they reflect and underline the whole Colefax & Fowler approach towards the decoration of houses. We believe that nature and natural forms are a wonderful and endless source of inspiration and that the timeless and apparently untouched mood in the decoration of old houses is as fitting a background in which to live as can be devised. The painting schemes of the Colefax & Fowler decorators, to which antiques and pictures are added, create a depth and authority which can only be achieved by this level of corporate talent.

ABOVE AND LEFT: TWO OIL
paintings of large Delft
tulipières filled, as they should
be, with tulips; some are the
'Parrot' variety.

TWO OF A SET OF FIVE BIRD watercolours. In the eighteenth and nineteenth centuries the study of nature was central to many people's lives. Birds, flowers and the countryside were major sources of inspiration and appeared in many forms in the decoration of their houses. George Oakes's birds owe much to the many volumes of eighteenth-century engravings and to such artists as Samuel Dixon, who went as far as embossing his paper to give his subjects the illusion of three-dimensional form.

DESIGN FOR A HAND PAINTED silk cushion cover.

A PAIR OF OCTAGONAL FLOWER pictures inspired by pole-screen frames.

CHAPTER 6

Colour, Pattern and Print

OPPOSITE: LADY ANNABEL Goldsmith's bedroom. The way the full-blooded 'Roses and Pansies' chintz covers everything in this eighteenth-century room shows how the fabric was sometimes used in the past.

P ATTERN, ITS SCALE AND BALANCE, IS THE MEANS THAT A decorator has to give coherence and rhythm to a room. The stylistic approach may be academic, disciplined or exuberant. Equally, it may break all the rules and just be intuitively visual. Success is not achieved by an exact adherence to any prescribed formula but, as with all creative expression, by flair and imagination. John Fowler's wonderful sense of colour and his inclination towards the lighter and simpler fabrics on which to print patterns, as well as the assurance with which he mixed them, were his particular strengths. It was the rare freshness of his approach, in marked contrast to the prevailing fashion for dour damasks and enriched Chippendale set in over-serious interiors, that was destined to exert such influence.

An approach to pattern and colour has to be decided upon at an early stage in decorating. Many aspects of a house and, more specifically, the room and furniture to be used within it should influence this choice. More than anything else, the determining factor will be the dominating period or style. Where the contents are more eclectic, however, it is often possible to define some sort of stylistic average or

RIGHT: THIS DECORATION began with the blue Mauny wallpaper 'Rayure et Corail'. Other blues and ribbon patterns have been worked into the scheme, such as the chintz on the *chaise longue* and the 'Roses and Ribbons' carpet.

theme which can be used as a starting point. This may be found, for example, in the relationship between a particular piece of furniture and the architecture of the house and room, or it could be provided by an entirely visual connection between the colours of a painting and those echoed in a carpet. From these considerations a palette of colours and a scale of pattern should emerge.

The size of a room also plays a part. All pattern and architectural detail should be determined by a room's height and not by its length or breadth. Exceptions to this rule can be made where the architectural character is very 'tough', as in some sixteenth- and seventeenth-century buildings with low ceilings. In these circumstances, the scale of patterns and furniture can be much larger than the height of the room would suggest. In fact, it is not a bad general rule to overscale rather than underscale, as this tends to make a room more memorable.

It is also important to note the room's aspect. Is it dark or light? Does it face south, west or north? The answers will all have a bearing on how the room is perceived and, in turn, on the choice of patterns and colours. Finally, the room's function and therefore the sort of atmosphere that might be most compatible with its use have to be taken into account. For instance, a drawing room facing south on to a garden might be kept light in colour and the patterns might complement and reflect the joys of the summer outside. A dining room with a northerly aspect may well be treated with warm, rich colours

IN THIS DRESSING ROOM, A number of busy little patterns are given an appropriate scale by the use of a matching border on the base of the gathered pelmet and down the leading edges and base of the curtains.

THE RIBBONS AND BOWS GIVE these small pictures visual structure and pick up the blue of the 'Lyme Park' wallpaper.

which not only compensate for the colder daytime light, but also look glowingly hospitable by candlelight. Every room should be analysed individually before the choice is made.

The ultimate aim is to make sure that pattern, colours and tone tell a convincing story in relation to a room. They should combine with its contents and function to make sense on both an intellectual and a visual level. Fowler's frequent suggestion to new clients was this: 'Pig it [in the house] for a year before you make any final decisions, and then you will have a much clearer idea of how you want to use it, the best places to sit or put a desk and what sorts of colours and patterns you may prefer in certain rooms.' This was excellent advice but, in these frenzied times, is unlikely to be taken. If you have the opportunity to hang a length of wallpaper in a room in which you are proposing to use it, do so. You should certainly know by the end of two weeks whether you have made the right choice or not.

A WING CHAIR AT BADMINTON covered in the first printing of the chintz 'Old Rose with Fancy', with a patch of the new chintz on the arm.

RIGHT: THE USE OF CHINTZ IN the grand manner. Pelmets are caught at the face to represent festoons. The plain yellow shantung silk draw curtains have wide borders of the same chintz.

When John Fowler began decorating, he was constantly on the look-out for scraps of old wallpaper and fragments of fabric from which to produce certain designs. 'Old Rose' and 'Brompton Stock' are chintzes that were found by him in the archives of Warners in the 1950s and have become favourite designs used by the firm ever since. Originally, these antique pieces were collected as sources of inspiration. It was only later that Tom Parr and George Oakes began to use them as the basis of the fabric collections which have now been in regular production since 1968. Some of the wallpapers used in the early Colefax & Fowler days came from the archives of Coles, at their factory in Islington, where so many of our hand-blocked papers have been printed over the years. Others were found in country houses, the insides of cupboards, chests-of-drawers or wherever Fowler's insatiable curiosity led him. 'Berkeley Sprig', now the company's logo, was found as he pulled away at the old red silk damask that upholstered the walls of the Grand Saloon at 44 Berkeley Square, which he was redecorating. It is a charming design of bell-shaped flowers on a diaper trellis and was probably inspired by a late seventeenth- or early eighteenth-century embroidered quilt.

Currently, there is an ever-expanding need to produce more wallpapers and fabrics for a market that increasingly demands greater variety, volume and complexity. As a consequence, the pressure on

OPPOSITE: LADY RUPERT NEVILL'S use of the chintz 'Roses and Pansies' in the sitting room of her home, Horsted Place.

BELOW: A FEW OF OUR CHINTZ document pieces (from left to right). Top: 'Hampton', 'Bailey Rose'; bottom: 'Passion Flower', 'Bowood'.

the design studio has increased and with it the need for inventiveness. Papers are now designed to fulfil every specific need. Amongst the textured papers, which act as restful backgrounds, there are a number with particular period associations. 'Brook', for example, was developed from a French dress muslin dating from the second half of the nineteenth century with the scale of its pattern increased four times. 'Ledbury', with a trailing nasturtium pattern, was based on the lining of a small box, probably mid-nineteenth-century German.

Patterns on fabrics and papers reflect their period just as much as the style of furniture indicates its date. This is as evident in the drawing of a design as in the way it is coloured. By changing the scale and recolouring the design we can adjust these period associations. However, it can only be done with understanding as it is easy to lose the balance of colour by using alternatives inappropriately. If the wrong colours are used, all that inspired the original design will be lost. In a modern palette of colours there is often a tendency to eliminate the dull or ugly colour frequently present in old designs to add contrast and weight to the cleaner, lighter colours. Where this has been done the results are often over-sweet and effeminate; the marketplace is, unfortunately, only too full of such examples. Modern fabrics can also suffer from the reverse: when the fresher colours have been dropped, leaving nothing but the drab, the effect is sad. The best-designed fabrics depend upon a balance of light and dark, clean and ugly, for the results to be really satisfying.

THE ORIGINAL DOCUMENT PIECE of 'Boughton' chintz.

'BERKELEY SPRIG', THE ORIGINAL document on an example of the current paper.

LEFT: 'BERKELEY SPRIG' GIVES the appearance of a stencil design in this country house hall.

Small to medium-sized designs are produced by Colefax & Fowler for rooms of average proportions in which a definite pattern is sought. The collections include small-scale sprigs, vermicelli and medallion motifs, as well as a whole range of simple to complex stripes. Some of the medium-scale patterns, which look very definite in small rooms, will in large rooms become almost like a texture. Certain small- to medium-scale designs are also produced in such a way that whichever direction the paper is used – upsidedown, sideways or on a diagonal – the pattern will still look correct. Such designs are intended to encourage schemes of decoration that would normally be difficult, if not impossible, to carry out, for instance using patterns on ceilings or the reveals and soffits to dormer windows. Most of the small and medium designs are now produced in colourways that match up with the standard fabrics that the company produces; this helps to overcome the need for special printings. Likewise, paper borders are also produced so that smaller patterns can be 'finished off'. This is a way of giving the architecture of a room extra emphasis, often allowing a small wallpaper design to look correct in a room in which it might otherwise be dismissed.

Large-scale papers such as our 'Double Damask', a tough design that has a textured ground like a distressed fresco, are very suitable for late seventeenth- and early eighteenth-century rooms and those that call for a certain boldness. Others are lighter in feeling and based on French late eighteenth-century damasks, where flowers and leaves in soft whites delicately trace their way across faded grounds of blue, pink or pale stone.

ABOVE: A LARGE-SCALE DAMASK wallpaper in sienna on a yellow ground was used as a background to this nineteenth-century four-poster bed with its rich crewelwork hangings.

When very luxurious wallpapers are required, most of the Colefax & Fowler decorators still turn to the French wallpaper firm Mauny. This tradition was started by John Fowler in 1934, when he was introduced to its founder, André Mauny. He was so impressed by the glories of the rich, hand-blocked designs, mostly dating from the late eighteenth century through to the middle of the nineteenth century, that he never ceased to use them for both informal and grand circumstances. There is an extremely pretty example in yellow and grey in a room that he decorated for his friend, Mrs Joan Dennis. In Buckingham Palace 'Frise Geraldine' was hung in a dark red colourway. Another of his favourite patterns, known as 'Primavères' – a large-scale flower and leaf design forming serpentine shapes – could be seen at Notley Abbey in Oxfordshire and in Fowler's own home, the Hunting Lodge.

THIS GROUND-FLOOR LONDON apartment uses two chintzes designed to team together. Both have the same stripe and moiré background, but the flowers on each are of a different scale.

LEFT: OUR 'DOUBLE DAMASK' wallpaper is a robust design which perfectly suits this hall with its tough early eighteenth-century furniture.

Chintz was much favoured by John Fowler and has remained a major source of the firm's inspiration ever since. Besides being widely used by the decorators in their work, it occupies a great deal of the studio's creative effort. The designs are either originals or adaptations from documents from which various colourways are produced.

Chintz is a printed cotton fabric which is subsequently glazed to enhance its look. Its origins are Indian and it reached its height of popularity in the eighteenth and early nineteenth centuries. The original designs were all floral as they were taken from the Indian Tree of Life motif. Through English interpretation this gave rise to all sorts of naturalistic forms, such as sprigs, garlands and bouquets of flowers. After the introduction of copper roller printing around 1815 the range of picturesque designs that have come to epitomize idyllic country house existence was vastly expanded. By the end of the nineteenth century, however, fashion had changed and there was a preference for richer, heavier, darker cloths that seemed in keeping with Queen Victoria's mourning at the passing of her consort.

John Fowler's taste for this fabric emerged principally from his preference for things that were light in feeling, had romantic charm about them and were unpretentious. Chintz, with its worn, barely discernible garlands of flowers and prettily painted cartouches, fitted in perfectly with his love of George III and Regency painted furniture. Together they combined to celebrate the life he loved: the country, gardens and the roses that grew there. Striped varieties of rose were his favourites and he would often return from weekends with some bloom to paint or simply to have at hand. 'Rosa Mundi' is a chintz reflecting his study of this flower.

In the early 1930s a few decorators had rediscovered the potential of chintz. Elsie de Wolfe in America was one who recognized the informal charm of this pretty and colourful fabric; the Hon Mrs Guy Bethell, who owned the influential decorating firm Eldens and was a friend of John Fowler's, was another. In Edwardian houses, they were known as calendered chintzes, not because they were changed (as is sometimes thought) in the spring and autumn, but because they were glazed in a calendering machine to a burnished finish. These fabrics were often used as everyday slip-covers to match curtains, a sort of 'day-time wear' for upholstery, not to be considered for rooms of real importance which contained good pictures and furniture. What Colefax & Fowler did in the early days was to elevate chintz to acceptability; it had then truly come of age and today is used extensively. Grandly draped beds and curtains are contrast bound or perhaps edged with more elaborate trimmings, but the cut and the conception are full of imagination. When the line of upholstery is emphasized by contrast piping, it is given a classic formality. Walls are also upholstered in chintz and trimmed with braid so that the whole room becomes an acclamation of the fabric's design. The use of these chintzes is endless: they can be floral or geometric, large in scale or small, passive and subordinate or lavish. But whatever the design, the feel of the fabric is crisp and the look fresh. The extraordinary growth in the popularity of this fabric in the last two decades is testament to the pleasure it gives.

Although there are no hard and fast rules, it is not a good idea to put a chintz with a chintz unless you are looking for a deliberately random effect, and then it is best to put a small-scale chintz with one of a larger scale. If you want to use chintz, use a lot of it. Other subordinate patterns could be in linen, a *bouclé* or a gauffraged *velour de lin* on which a design has been stamped. If you choose plain linens, then contrast piping will break up the form and add visual interest. Self-patterned weaves and checks which have a geometric structure contrast well with the natural forms of most chintz patterns. The balance of colours is crucial – warm with cool, sharp with soft, light with dark, pretty with ugly. All are important, in order that the whole room can become an expansion of the harmony found in the chintz itself.

Besides chintzes, there are many other fabrics that can be used, some of which we have developed ourselves such as the self-patterned plain materials, hand-woven checks and stripes, and printed linens. More recently, the collections have included *bouclés*, which are machine-made tapestry weaves, and some pure wool damasks that evoke the mid nineteenth century. These are usually coloured to coordinate with one another and fit the precepts that we have about

A COLOURBOARD FOR A bedroom scheme showing all the fabrics, the carpet and the trimmings.

THE COMPLETED BEDROOM looking through into the dressing room.

OPPOSITE: EVERYTHING IN THIS bedroom is covered in 'Old Rose' chintz, except one big easy chair, its run-up stool and the embroidered muslin lining to the bed drapes.

colour and its use. In principle, these follow our attitude towards paintwork. Colours that are too new, too bright or too clean obstruct the harmony with old rugs, pictures and antiques. To us, the illusion of the passing of time is the co-ordinating factor. Our whites are never white but softened down; blacks are never black but bleached and warm, and all the colours in between have apparently been faded by the strong sunlight of long summer days.

Amongst the other fabrics that we continue to use, some are old favourites of John Fowler's, such as the silk damask called 'Valancy'. Most silk damasks in current use, with their thick forms of symmetrical acanthus, owe their origins to the Renaissance. 'Valancy' is different in that it is light in feeling with freely formed motifs of pomegranates and leaves: off-whites on the prettiest grounds of oyster, pale cerulean, pink, heart-of-lettuce green and a colour known as 'Petworth gold'. This fabric strikes a balance between richness and modesty that is particularly pleasing. We also use velvets of cotton, silk or mohair, but they are often 'gauffraged'. This method of stamping a design into a fabric is particularly effective when the cloth has a nap; the light then throws the pattern into relief. The subtle design is not immediately apparent; it is both discreet and intensely rich.

Toile de Jouy, like chintz, is a material with a certain simplicity about it. Unlike chintz, it is a single colour print on off-white, unglazed calico. For over 200 years it has been printed outside Paris at Jouy. The fabric has a unique quality as only engraved designs are printed on to it; these are generally in blue or red but sometimes in other colours. The designs themselves are very pictorial, and typical are French pastoral scenes and Chinoiserie fantasies. Stranger subjects are also to be found where engraved plates from newspapers and broadsheets proclaiming outstanding events, such as Montgolfier's first balloon flight, are employed. 'Décor', a large overall floral design from France, is one of the most impressive. Its finely etched lines produce a great variety of tones in the leaves, flowers and branches, giving it great presence. It is, however, less demanding than that of a polychrome design. *Toile de Jouy* fabrics make an ideal background and for this reason they have traditionally been used in France in a particular way. Everything in the room is covered in it: the walls, the beds and their attendant drapes, the curtains, the blinds and the slipcovers. The simplicity of the overall effect is startling, and serves to show how a single concept used to the full is often the most dramatic.

The subject of pattern in rooms is bound to be governed by personal taste. However, there are certain general observations that can be made. Single patterns on fabrics, such as damasks or chintzes, can be used effectively all over a room, even as upholstery on walls if desired. This conforms to seventeenth- and eighteenth-century practice both in England and on the Continent. In the early nineteenth century, self-patterned plains, typically small neo-Classical rosettes and stripes, became fashionable. The splendid draperied effects of many of these Regency interiors have hardly ever been equalled. Certain English and Continental rooms were completely tented, with the furniture upholstered to match.

IN EARLY SEVENTEENTH-century architecture, as well as that of the nineteenth century, a density of decoration is often the most satisfactory. This style relies for its effect on the layering of pattern and detail on yet further pattern. Rich antique embroidery can be used against nineteenth-century Willement wallpapers, complicated Jacquards and screens of various sorts. The principal aim is to create an atmosphere of a dark and mysterious sort – in many ways a development from and reaction to the purity of John Fowler's style in the early years.

Mixing lots of different patterns and textures is currently common practice. The inspiration for this comes from two sources. The first is the influence of interiors of the mid to late nineteenth century, when a taste for the exotic came into fashion. Persian, Oriental and Zeigler rugs were then freely mixed in with elaborately woven door curtains, stamped or cut velvets, needlework chairs and tapestry hangings. In addition, very complicated Jacquard weaves figured prominently, often with strong Gothic or Renaissance echoes. The furniture, which was almost without exception historical revival in design, was as highly worked. This style of room relies for its effect on layer upon layer of embellishment, pattern and detail; some large and passive, others small and intense. Surfaces with a sheen are juxtaposed with others that are matt and recessive. The principal rule here is the control of the tones. From light to dark, from strong to mute, they all have to blend, because mystery and atmosphere are at the core of this approach. Nothing whiter than the ground colour of Imari ware, nothing blacker than the burnished ebony of *boulle* should be considered. This is a background for ormolu, *objets vertus* and the rich patterns of *pietra dura* half seen in subdued light. Geoffrey Bennison was the doyen of this particular approach to decoration, and the influence of both his antique shop in Pimlico and the private houses that he decorated was immense. As a result many decorators today in England, Europe and America are familiar with this profusion of pattern and subdued colour, supported by huge pieces of mysterious dark furniture.

The second influence for this practice is that of grand English country houses as they were found at the end of the Second World War: not the formal, controlled interiors of their eighteenth-century conception, but as succeeding generations had adapted them to their own changing requirements. This mood was characterized by comfortable chairs, useful tables piled high with books, lamps to read by, drinks tables groaning with bottles and garden flowers in large vases. The new interpretation is one of gentle informality where plain and patterned fabrics look as if they have found their way into a room by accident rather than by anything more deliberate. The apparent visual ease with which these interiors are created belie the subtlety of their planning. The deceptive simplicity gives them a look that is in fact difficult to emulate.

CHAPTER 7 Upholstery and Soft Furnishing

ABOVE: THE GROUND FLOOR hall of this Wiltshire rectory has been treated like a small sitting room, with a comfortable jumble of possessions that one associates with the best of English country houses.

RIGHT: THE QUEEN ANNE WING chair at Haseley Court presiding idiosyncratically over a regiment of William IV morocco leather chairs.

OPPOSITE: THE FIRST FLOOR landing of the Wiltshire rectory. The combination of pictures, prints and plenty of fabric, shrouding the window and on the upholstery, adds to the sense of comfort and luxury.

JOHN FOWLER'S PREFERENCE FOR MIXING ALL SORTS OF UPHOLSTERY AND other seat furniture was based on the comfortable jumble that he invariably found in the country houses on which he worked. Both he and Nancy Lancaster liked the informality and element of surprise that could be achieved by unusual juxtapositions. For example, in the dining room at Haseley, Nancy Lancaster's Oxfordshire home, a Queen Anne wing chair presides idiosyncratically at the head of the table in its chintz slip-cover over a regiment of rather correct William IV morocco leather chairs which seem to wear their brass lifting handles like epaulettes.

Variety in scale and purpose of seating is also much more practical because we ourselves come in various shapes and sizes. Deep-sprung armchairs, higher, firmer, open armchairs, small upholstered spoon-backs like our 'Friar's' chair, at its best in stamped or 'gauffraged' velour, combine together happily. One or two sofas and perhaps another chair to match, not in style but in fabric, is the sort of formula often employed: a mix and match, an interplay of fabrics and colours. A theme with variations and twists, with comfortable down-filled cushions, gives emphasis or counterpoint to the colours used while all remains in harmony.

The design and construction of the shapes and detail of upholstery are fundamental to much of our work, due to the example set by John Fowler. Years ago an actor, whose name I have long forgotten, told me this story to illustrate the decorator's passionate interest in the way such things were put together. They were sharing rooms at a time when Fowler was at the very beginning of his career. He came home with a pair of eighteenth-century curtains with some sort of elaborate heading; he proceeded to unpick them entirely and then remake them, assembling each detail exactly as it had been, so that he might understand the cut, the line and how such effects were achieved. After the war, Mary, Duchess of Buccleuch remembers how Fowler took the time to show her own work people at Boughton how to upholster some French chairs correctly in the French manner.

Fowler taught us to look for classic form. Today this is achieved through much trial and error because the development of a design is a difficult balance between comfort and line. The line of upholstery is given emphasis by contrast piping and binding. Fowler may not have invented this, but in any event he made such wide use of it, at a time when it was almost unseen, that one might be forgiven for assuming so; there are many precedents of contrast edging on Regency costume which may well have been his inspiration. Eighteenth- and nineteenth-century clothes, every bit as much as rosettes, bows and other document trimmings, were of such interest to him that he could be seen transfixed, with glasses pushed up on his forehead, peering at the way seamstresses had finished off their work.

THE QUEEN ANNE NEEDLEWORK wing chair has been edged with a short loopwool fringe which is appropriate to upholstery of this date.

LEFT: ATTENTION TO DETAIL IS evident in the upholstery of this sofa. Contrast piping defines its lines and the gathered fabric skirt, with contrast binding, has a tiny stand-up frill. Cushions look best and are most comfortable when filled generously, like these, with pure down.

When we upholster today piping may be made from dyed silk or cotton ottoman, depending on the upholstery fabric against which it is to be seen. This is cut on the cross to give it the appearance of a fine cord. Alternatively, the same cotton or linen as the main fabric may be used for piping in colours two tones darker, lighter or perhaps sharper to give the appropriate accent. Piping is used on cushions, squabs, slip-covers, in fact on all sorts of upholstery, as it is one of the simplest and most effective ways of giving a design distinction. When a very simple, understated effect is sought, upholstery is self-piped; case-covers for dining chairs or *bergères* can be treated in this way.

Occasionally, Fowler's predilection for the simple found a response in the most unlikely places. In the case of Lady Ancaster, it

THESE FINE QUALITY ENGLISH eighteenth-century chairs have been given further distinction by a short fringe and a double row of nails.

practically upstaged his own taste. While he was working on her two remarkable houses, Grimsthorpe Castle in Lincolnshire and Drummond Castle in Scotland, she insisted that the lampshades be knocked up in card and that the slip-covers fit rather badly, 'big and baggy, as if made by housemaids'. He was immensely amused by this request, but fully approved of the mood that would be achieved by it.

Depending on what effect is required, the finish of upholstery may be treated in a variety of ways. A bullion fringe, a style prevalent in 1830s and 1840s furnishings, makes a strong masculine statement. A skirt can be left plain or gathered and contrast bound in various ways; it may even have a gathered stand-up frill at the top and a frill at the bottom that are both contrast bound. Nowadays, we sometimes omit the skirt; the legs are left bare, ebonized or polished. The bottom edge is then trimmed with braid. This can either be 'close-nailed', where the nails touch, or 'space-nailed', where the nails are about 25 mm apart. Nailing is most often adopted when heavier fabrics such as *bouclés*, leather or antique needlework are chosen as a covering.

ABOVE: THIS GATHERED, embroidered muslin lampshade, looking like an old-fashioned housemaid's pinafore, has a delightful femininity.

ABOVE RIGHT: AN ODD assortment of upholstery in a bedroom is always appealing. The elaborate headings to the curtains and the scheme's coordinated colours give conviction to the room's contents.

111

When it came to the upholstery of good antique furniture, John Fowler insisted upon the correct method for each particular chair: round, domed, softer forms for eighteenth-century Continental chairs and a harder, squarer look for English furniture, as can be seen in the engravings from Chippendale's *The Gentleman & Cabinet Maker's Director*. The backs of chairs and the various ways of treating them also interested him. Infinite care would be taken in order that the correct bows or tufts were chosen to go with various fabrics instead of the buttons which are still commonly used as a lazy substitute. However, Fowler was no pedant and we were sometimes taught that rules could be broken. When a large man's open armchair came into the shop covered in its original, but much distressed, morocco leather upholstery, with one or two of the original buttons missing (the buttons in this case being correct), his solution was a bold one. He had the morocco leather restored as expected, but removed all the leather buttons and replaced them with tiny, deep red silk tufts. The result was stately.

In England truly comfortable upholstery was not developed until the second quarter of the nineteenth century, although one does come across comfortable settees of an earlier date. These, having one great feather-and-down squab on the seat and being deep enough for lots of extra plump cushions to support the back, are an exception. Most Georgian furniture was much more austere, having webbing, horsehair and wadding. It was with the introduction of springs and deep padding around 1840 that things changed and new ideas of luxury developed. In the pursuit of an overall mood that is informal and relaxed, an antique chair covered in its existing fabric can sometimes be used as it has been found. It is then carefully taken apart, restored and reassembled. From time to time a good eighteenth-century arm or library chair, which has some time in the past been incorrectly upholstered with a sprung seat, might be acquired. It is probable that the

A SELECTION OF SOME OF Fowler's trimmings. They all show his feeling for detail which is much more akin to costume than to furnishing, but in the eighteenth century there was little distinction between the two.

LEFT AND OPPOSITE: A TESTER at Sudeley Castle. The pretty green leaf chintz has been contrast bound at its gathered top edge and finished with a two-tone linen fan edging at the bottom.

adaptation has made it much more comfortable, and so we leave it as it is. The antique trade would certainly disapprove of such a practice, but many a room can lose something of its appeal by an overabundance of too much correct furniture. The final decision is likely to be governed by the quality of the antique and the priorities of the owner.

In his treatment of curtains and drapery for beds Fowler was supreme. He raised the making of curtains into a real art by introducing a spirited lightness into their conception and cut. This he was able to do because he understood their design and construction in terms both of detail and creation in a way that had few parallels at the time. In France, perhaps the most sophisticated country in the world with regard to interior decoration, there was no equivalent figure and so the understanding of elaborate draperies went into decline. The early nineteenth-century neo-Classical glories by such upholsterers as the Parisian d'Hallevant were all but forgotten. Even today, Madeleine Castaing, the inspired French decorator, may be an exception, but her influence is confined to the sophisticated few who share her passion for the autumnal days of the French Empire and the *intimiste* mood of the Belle Epoque.

SOME OF THE TRIMMINGS which the firm of B. A. Clarke produced for Fowler. Guilloche and Gothic gimps (at the top); tassels and rosettes (on the right); and complicated fringes, including the pretty yellow example looking like wistaria (left of centre).

114

Fowler's general approach, which we still reflect, was that curtains, like costume, are best designed and detailed in a manner that is subordinate to the line. If the drawing of a design is good, the cut executed with conviction and all is made well, simple trimmings can be wonderfully effective. An interest in very complex trimmings, however, has always been strong as Fowler, an inveterate hoarder, had built up a large reference of such items. Through B.A. Clarke, a firm which was kept running entirely by him on the manufacture of such trimmings, he was able to have a great variety of types made. Complicated fly fringes, Gothic and guilloche gimps, tassels of innumer-

TOP: CURTAINS TWO TONES deeper than the walls. The swagged headings are caught by *choux* and finished with an elaborate guilloche-headed silk fringe.

ABOVE: A BLUE SILK SCALLOPED tieback edged with a yellow silk harlequin trimming. The blue matches the curtain lining.

ABOVE RIGHT: AT RADBOURNE Hall, Derbyshire, Fowler's elaborate pennant-style window draperies look positively heraldic. The red, lining the curtains, is also visible in the centre *choux* and on the tails; at the outer edge the headings are held by bows.

able sorts were tried, developed and perfected. The silhouettes of the turned wooden moulds for the tassels were given as much thought as the colouring of the yarns and their interaction with one another. Having access to so many fine trimmings at Colefax & Fowler has encouraged us to understand them as beautiful work in their own right. More importantly, we have seen how they can be used as additional enrichment to the most glorious draperies and upholstery. Through a familiarity over the years with these fringes and elaborate furnishings we have gained unrivalled experience in using them with confidence.

As a less expensive alternative to woven trimmings, complicated effects can be created simply out of fabric. Having their parallels in the details of eighteenth-century costume, they have added much to the firm's present-day vocabulary. Ruffles and flounces are still as much used as in Fowler's day, as well as scalloped and pinked edges whose effects are produced on old, specially designed machines. Ruched bands are used for pelmets and occasionally tie backs; bows and *choux* provide luxurious points of emphasis. However elaborate the conception of these details, Fowler always kept them for the appropriate place, to establish the right mood. It is therefore at houses with the scale of Radburne Hall, in Derbyshire, or in the vast drawing room window in Pauline de Rothschild's set in the Albany, London, that the grandeur of such effects can be seen at their best.

It is curtains using such trimmings and complicated effects on elaborately dressed headings for which Colefax & Fowler are best known. Together with John Fowler's views on the painting of houses,

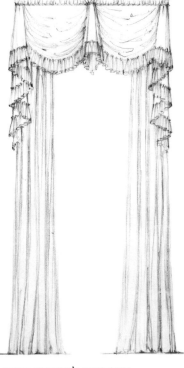

JOHN FOWLER'S PROPOSED curtain design for the best bedroom at Chevening, Kent. Grand yet restrained, the headings are simply finished with gathered frills.

IT IS FOR ELABORATE AND beautifully dressed curtains such as these that Colefax & Fowler are best known.

they represent his most significant bequest to us. Extravagantly conceived drapes to windows and on beds have always been in evidence and there are many eighteenth- and nineteenth-century examples to which one can turn for inspiration, although most of them have lost their line over the years through destruction by the light, dusting and cleaning, or even by the lack of it. The more elaborate draperies of the first quarter of this century were uninspired, flat in look and offered little by way of example. It was Fowler's sympathy for the essence of the late eighteenth century, the period he loved best, that set the tone. His shapes were full, his line elegant, and he was confident. Whether his curtains were austere, had swags, bows or fringes, or were made with or without tails, they were always handled with discrimination. The decoration and the scale of architecture always had to be appropriate. If a window demanded a particular solution, the curtains were devised to match it.

IN THIS WINDOW, THE BLUE festooned blinds complete the effect of a swathed and draped bay. The blinds are set half way down the window to filter the daytime light.

At Ditchley Park, in Oxfordshire, the windows in the hall required a severe treatment, but with some sort of headings to the curtains. The windows, however, had no deadlight, that is, the space between the top of the window architrave and the cornice. Any pelmet, therefore, would have reduced the light into the room, which was to be avoided. Nancy Lancaster had a sketch of a curtain heading originally used by her old friend Edward Knoblock that seemed to suggest the answer. A false pelmet was attached to the curtains so that when they were drawn the pelmets followed. During the day the windows were fully exposed and at night they had the dressed look that suited the room best. This solution has since been successfully used on many occasions.

Uppark was one of the first houses regularly visited by John Fowler. The bleached ivory whites and the flecked gilding of the Saloon epitomized the eighteenth-century spirit that was always to haunt him. He was particularly struck by the yellow damask curtains, being of a type with which he was not familiar at the time. They were in fact festoon curtains, the design of which he was later to use in a variety of ways. The earliest examples were those he made for Lord Wilton and hung in the Saloon at Ramsbury Manor, in Wiltshire. It took much trial and error to get them hanging and working properly, for at the time nobody was quite sure how they should be made to operate. Fowler was perhaps the first decorator to reintroduce and use them in this century.

Recently, festoon curtains have had too much exposure; they are often badly proportioned and inappropriately used, which has done much to damage their appeal. When the architecture of windows has interesting features, such as finely carved architraves, deep shuttered reveals or where a window seat can be added, festoon curtains can be used to particularly good effect. Moreover, they leave the architecture

A STRAIGHT GATHERED PELMET. For rooms of modest proportions a simple window treatment is preferable. Here the straight profile of this valance is ideally suited to this eighteenth-century bedroom. The bottom edge of the valance and the leading and bottom edges of the curtains are finished with a double pinked frill.

SIMPLE GATHERED CURTAINS IN a hall give a comfortable furnished look to the space; the dog anyhow feels perfectly at home here.

118

TOP: A FOUR-POSTER BED WITH lace hangings. The severity of the line is appropriate to the simplicity of the posts and the profile of the tester frame.

ABOVE: THE INSIDE OF THE tester showing the sunburst gathering from a central *chou*. The curtains and the valance are finished with a linen fan edging.

of a room less cluttered. In heavier fabrics they can be lined, interlined and finished with a bold bullion fringe. With lighter fabrics they can be simply trimmed or, with the addition of a gathered frill, be given a more elaborate line and look. Their headings can be gathered, pencil- or box-pleated, but they look best when used with a shaped giltwood pelmet. The example of the festoon curtains in the green drawing room at Clandon Park, in Surrey, looks especially fine.

In plainer rooms of smaller size, curtains of a more restrained nature are recommended. The most simple are those with plain pinched pleats, or *tête de Versailles* headings as they are sometimes called; they can also be gathered, which is slightly untidier in mood. They are usually contrast bound, but alternatively a braid can be used. If the architecture has the sort of weight that is associated with the seventeenth or the late nineteenth century, a more robust design is required. Here large poles and rings – sometimes metal, sometimes polished or painted wood with carved and gilded finials – should be considered. As the architectural scale increases, so must the scale in the treatment of the curtains' details. Getting it right is simply a matter of balance.

Beds are, and always have been, the supreme extravagance of the

119

upholsterer's art. The great beds of the seventeenth and eighteenth centuries were not only the most costly single items in any house of distinction, but they were also seen to reflect a family's status and pride. In decorating bedrooms, an elaborate bed has the advantage of elevation, which is of value when it comes to creating a sense of balance in a room. Window curtains tend to look uncomfortable when the bed is a huge horizontal slab of anything up to 2 metres square; with a single bed the proportions are more manageable. It is also important that the mattress should be a reasonable height off the ground, approximately 70 to 75 cm. Until this century, beds were generally

A SERPENTINE CURTAIN
valance. Serpentine or arched
forms of curtain headings are
best in rooms of moderate
proportions where a straight
line would seem too
understated. Here the heading
has been simply gathered but
the base, along with the
leading edge and bottom of
the curtains, has double
gathered frills, pinked and
scalloped. The plain blue
chintz of the underfrill picks
up the colour in the pattern of
the main fabric.

made to a sensible height, so that when you are lying back on two pillows your head is at the same level as someone sitting in an adjacent chair, which is a reasonably equitable arrangement. A bedside table is then at the right height and you can actually get a proper view out of the windows instead of seeing nothing but the sky, as is the case with all modern beds. In cottages, the scale of the bedrooms and their windows alleviates the need for a draped bed, which would be inappropriate in the circumstances. Nevertheless, a simpler bed, whether in wood, iron or brass, should still stand at the correct height.

The designs of elaborately dressed beds take many forms, but they are all based on the idea of drapery hung from some type of canopy or tester covering all or part of the bed. The tester can be supported on posts, hung from the ceiling or be in the form of a small corona or crown. A particularly pretty example is the 'Polonaise' bed, with a corona centrally supported on four shaped arms. A number were used in England, and the Haseley bed in the 'Gothic Tracery' chintz is an elegant example. The treatment of tester beds is extremely wide; they can be severe and masculine with a straight silhouette, or they can be extravagant and feminine with swags, tails and elaborate trimmings. It is the house, the room and the decorations as a whole which are likely to determine the choice.

As a greater complexity has crept into decoration, so walls are upholstered more than before. This adds a richness to the quality of a room; the acoustics improve and the mood becomes authoritative. When damask is used the atmosphere is shadowed and enveloping; in the case of chintz the effect can be charming and light. Fabric can also be hung loosely, gentle folds falling from the cloakpins that hold it at the head. On occasion we tent whole rooms, and these usually look

IN MEDIEVAL AND TUDOR architecture fabric can be hung loosely over the walls from exposed iron hooks placed under a frieze. In early nineteenth-entury neo-Classical rooms brass or ormolu cloakpins are more appropriate.

BEDROOM WARDROBES AND cupboards can often be treated so that they tie in with the rest of the room's decoration. We sometimes design them with glazed or wire mesh doors behind which is gathered a fabric used elsewhere in the room.

best when everything is in one fabric. Carl Frederick Shinkel, the early nineteenth-century German architect, was the master of this device. There is also that inspired example of tented material in Queen Hortense's boudoir in her house in the Rue Cerutti, Paris. This is one of the most romantic early nineteenth-century rooms decorated in the neo-Classical taste.

Fabric, gathered or knife-pleated, is often applied to the back of cupboard doors with mesh grills. This allows the use of a fabric's design or colour already in the room to break up the visual mass of a piece of furniture that would otherwise be too dominating or heavy. Glazed doors to a dressing room or bathroom can also be softened by fabric used in this way. In the last decade, more contrived decoration has emerged to make up for the loss of quality in the pictures and furniture that are now available. While the scope for decoration has increased, it is only the limit of our imagination that holds us back. When one sees what has been achieved by those who commit themselves totally to the pursuit of an idea, using the upholsterer's art as a medium, one has to conclude that the loss of great possessions is perhaps not such a loss after all.

IN SMALL SPARE BEDROOMS, where a clothes press or wardrobe would seem too dominant, a small tented wardrobe can solve the problem. It looks amusing and, in a corner, takes up less space.

RIGHT: AN INGENIOUS BUILT-IN wardrobe using a copy of a pelmet that John Fowler painted in his early days. The chintz curtains with rope tiebacks complete the effect.

123

CHAPTER 8   # Floors and Floorcoverings

A MARBLE FLOOR WITH SLATE or stone sets is very eighteenth-century in spirit and is particularly suitable for halls.

A COTTAGE ENTRANCE HALL with its recently laid stone floor. The secret of this rustic flooring is to make sure that old slabs are used and that they are as large as possible.

OPPOSITE: IN HOUSES OF AN early date, where robust details are much in evidence, rush matting looks perfect. It has all the strength of character associated with stone or old floorboards but is soft underfoot and dampens sound. It should be watered from time to time to prevent it from becoming too brittle.

To HAVE ANY REAL QUALITY INTERIORS NEED TO BE SUPPORTED BY good architecture. The materials used and the grammar of the details are more than a background; they are the basic plot through which the story of the decoration is woven. Whereas walls and woodwork are subject to adaptation and repainting, floors, when uncarpeted, remain unaltered. It is the robustness of the materials associated with floors and their use which gives them their permanence. As they are the most constant of backgrounds, much thought should be given to their choice.

The patination of a natural material through years of wear and tear can contribute much to a room's identity. Old York stone, honed white marble with slate sets, brick floors or ancient quarry tiles all possess durable and timeless characteristics, qualities which are deeply satisfying in an age which appears to be committed to the idea that change is progress. These materials are at their best where formality takes precedence over comfort, such as entrance halls and, on occasion, dining rooms; use can then be made of the architectural patterns that are associated with these sorts of materials. They are appropriate in large country kitchens, conservatories and terraces or indeed in any room where their resilient qualities can be put to best use.

125

Plain boarded floors are a wonderful surface as they are warm, substantial and reassuringly familiar. They also provide the perfect background for old rugs and carpets. Old wood floors are preferable; new floors can very rarely recreate the richness of the originals. The types of wood that look best are oak, chestnut or elm; boards should be cut as wide as possible and the arrises or edges slightly rounded to suggest a certain age. Random widths are also sometimes preferred because there are many historical precedents. New floorboards can be given a patination by being knocked about a bit, stained, coloured or left plain, as best suits the room's decoration; finally they should be wax polished. When the floors are light in colour, we tend to prefer a wax finish that has a semi-matt surface, as this corresponds more closely to the eighteenth-century dry, scrubbed look. If a deep, almost black floor is wanted it should be stained, waxed and then burnished. The days are gone when silversand was used for cleaning floorboards and herbs such as rosemary, thyme, and lavender were brushed on to keep the rooms sweet and drive the flies and moths away. Today, this is impractical; instead we wax our floors and use bowls of pot-pourri for fragrance.

PARQUETRY FLOORS PROVIDE AN ideal background for rugs. This Bessarabian flatweave rug suits the proportions of this hall to perfection.

A SIMULATED PARQUETRY floor. This form of decoration is best on chestnut or elm so that an amusing interplay is created by the natural figuring of the wood and the stained or painted patterns.

126

Painted floors are really a *trompe l'oeil* technique in which there is no real attempt to create the belief that the boarded floors on which the work is carried out looks like stone, parquetry or carpet. It is a humorous device whereby there is a constant tease in the interplay between the boards and the decoration. The idea is more Continental and American than English and looks best where the walls are also treated in the same rather whimsical manner. It is sometimes used in smaller rooms to suggest deliberate illusion of misplaced grandeur, as it creates an opportunity to use a few good pieces of furniture with more modest things.

ABOVE RIGHT: RUGS LOOK BEST of all on old polished floorboards, where the contrast of textures is most evident.

Rush, coconut and sisal matting are also excellent floor finishes. The texture is tough and fibrous, the colours are striated in a way that is reminiscent of wood. Laid well with a traditional hair underfelt, they have the advantage of being warm and acoustically good while having the quality of a natural material. As John Fowler did in the old days, we still use matting today. Country cottages, studies and garden rooms such as Fowler's own at Odiham, benefit hugely from the simplicity of its spirit. The rush variety is particularly suitable in early houses where the architecture is robust. Fowler's use of rush matting in the Long Gallery at Sudbury Hall, in Derbyshire, is a notable example. Visually, rugs and antique carpets look very good against matting. In the larger and more formal houses of a later date this material may seem too rustic, and so self-patterned and small-patterned carpets can be used as an alternative, sometimes with the addition of a border to give an architectural emphasis to the floor.

Over the years Colefax & Fowler have developed a whole range of such carpets. They are Brussels weave in construction and have a traditional mood that can take rugs on them very well. Some are designed specifically for this purpose; the 'Flemings' carpet is one

127

example. The general consensus is that small patterns help to overcome the blandness of plain carpeting and that the tougher texture of a loop pile looks more satisfactory. The patterns should be kept small and passive so as not to compete with the rugs.

In the first half of this century Brussels weave carpets had ceased to be used as there was no interest in their particular texture or the patterns associated with them. The first two to be reintroduced, by John Fowler in the late 1930s, were 'Mossy', a dense overall design of tree forms with cottagey overtones, and 'Medallion', a small repeat Classical quatrefoil design. A fragment of 'Medallion' was found by Fowler in the archives at Crossley's, the carpet manufacturers, who reacted

BELOW: 'ROCKSAVAGE' – A vigorous, masculine design with William IV associations.

with some astonishment to the interest shown in such an old-fashioned fragment. They admitted that the looms still existed although they had been out of use for decades. Much encouragement and persuasion was needed before the right worsted wool yarn could be produced and the carpet rewoven. Now, thirty years later, these Brussels weave carpets are used by decorators everywhere. In structure they have a tight loop pile in wool on a jute ground and are woven to the old standard 27 in (69 cm) width, with a variety of widths for borders.

Colefax & Fowler also introduced other *patera* designs as antique pieces came to light. Some came from archives or clients' houses; others were found in antique shops, often on pieces of furniture like bedsteps and the tops of old commodes. These fitted carpets with their borders running around a room have a very particular look which has become one of the hallmarks of a Colefax & Fowler interior. When

THE 'ROCKSAVAGE' CARPET HAS a strapwork design with a big repeat. It is eminently suitable in large-scale rooms where there is a strong early nineteenth-century atmosphere.

'STRAWBERRIES' DESIGNED BY John Fowler.

used as background carpets, the field of the design should be more neutral in colour and tone and the motifs controlled; but used in their own right, the colours can be more assertive so that the carpet becomes a major consideration in the way a room looks. The more elaborate Brussels weave patterns are always laid with borders designed to go with them. Large-scale carpets are chosen for large-scale rooms. Again, the scale should be determined by the room's height, as explained in Chapter 6.

The country house sale at Ashburnham Place, in Sussex, in 1950 was of special significance to those who were curious about the undisturbed mood of period houses. The house had been shut up for decades until it was unlocked and the sale of its contents took place; time had stood still and it had remained a tired beauty, witness to a life that had been lived in the first half of the nineteenth century. John Fowler and Nancy Lancaster bought a number of objects at this sale, amongst which were three colourways of the same carpet: one with a red ground, a second with a brown ground and a third with a blue ground. Today, most people would frown on the idea of using one carpet design in three colourways in the same house as being too easy a solution. The brown colourway of this old carpet with its matching border was later relaid in the Tobacco Bedroom at Haseley. 'Roses and Ribbons', as it was later called, was the first large-scale Brussels weave carpet to be acquired. The pattern of this 1830 design has a delightfully free rhythm of leaves and blooms that are abstractly scattered across the floor and evoke the typical country house atmosphere in which the gardens outside are echoed within. 'Roses and Ribbons' achieves that balance whereby the pattern has presence without taking over and therefore contributes to the importance of grand room, but in a manner that is 'well behaved'. This is the mark of a carpet design at its best but one that can easily be lost in any recolouring.

Inspired by this example, other carpets were also reproduced by the firm. 'Rocksavage' was found at Cholmondley Castle, in Cheshire, an example of very early nineteenth-century castle architecture, and presumably the carpet was designed around the same time. The 'Beaufort' design was acquired from Beaufort Castle, in Invernesshire (c. 1830). John Fowler then designed 'Strawberries', a charming late eighteenth-century pastiche of a strawberry plant in a large quatrefoil on a speckled ground. Later, a carpet called 'Turkish' was designed by George Oakes for more masculine rooms. It looks particularly good in a cut-pile finish when it corresponds closely to the mid nineteenth-century rugs that inspired it. More recently, other mid nineteenth-century designs have been found, one of medium scale called 'Persian flower' and another called 'Chester', whose large scale makes it suitable for use in the everincreasing number of rooms into which we have to place mid nineteenth-century furniture. All these carpets are rich and complex and reflect the current interest in forms of decoration that are more elaborate and dense.

Certain types of antique rugs and carpets have always been sought after by Colefax & Fowler because they have featured constantly in the country houses that have been such an inspiration to the firm. It is

THE BRUSSELS WEAVE CARPET 'Higford' is a small *patera* design and one of our most popular carpets. It comes with a guilloche border, which can be seen at the bottom of these stairs.

THE 'ROSES AND RIBBONS' Brussels weave carpet with its double guilloche border. This was the first of the large-scale Colefax designs.

129

their colours and scale that on so many occasions have germinated ideas for the decoration of rooms. To balance a room's colour scheme with a good rug can establish a unity in the decoration that is striking.

Large rugs have been used in country houses since the beginning of the seventeenth century and have been objects of great beauty in which their owners took considerable pride. The early Turkey work carpets, the English imitation of Persian or Oriental carpets, have all but worn out and disappeared. The eighteenth-century English needlework type, of which there are still a number in existence because they can always be repaired, have always been highly desir-

THE 'ROSES AND RIBBONS' hearth rug. This design is an early nineteenth-century pastiche produced by the Colefax & Fowler studio.

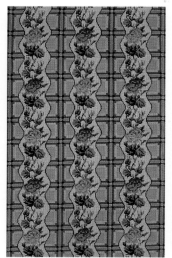

A NEEDLEWORK DOG RUG BASED on a late-nineteenth-century English hearth rug.

AN ENTRANCE HALL SHOWING A diagonal Portland stone floor with oak dividing strips and an oak border. This was inspired by the hall of a eighteenth-century French house.

able, but with the prices they fetch nowadays they are somewhat intimidating to walk on. Recently, a number of very good nineteenth-century needlework facsimiles have come on to the market, some made in India, others in Portugal. Colefax & Fowler have also produced some needlework rugs that evoke this spirit of nineteenth-century whimsy.

In the late eighteenth and early nineteenth centuries, pile carpets were produced by Wilton and Axminster and were in fairly common use. Initially, their design followed a Classical format quite like that of the French Savonneries. After the 1820s their design became more romantic and tended to adopt the glorious floral motifs that are associated with needlework rugs and the patterns on chintzes and china of the period. These colourful rugs, which celebrate the love of gardens and botanical decoration, fit perfectly with the firm's concept of design and wide use of romantic fabrics. Bessarabian rugs, although flat weave, are similar in that the motifs are often floral due, surprisingly, to the influence of French chintzes. The interpretation, however, is geometrically stylized, giving them considerable naive charm. The consequence of using rugs with this type of floral decoration is that the rooms assume an unabashed prettiness and, with the support of sympathetic decoration, can be as glorious as a Gertrude Jekyll garden.

From 1880 onwards Zeiglers and Heriz rugs became popular. The Zeiglers, made in Sultanabad, have traditional Persian motifs of abstract flowers, leaves and tendrils but are inclined to be softer in colour as they were woven for the European and American markets. The advantage of these rugs was that they could easily accommodate the greater degree of eclecticism which was finding its way into the furnishing of homes at that time. The Heriz rugs were coarsely woven but very hard wearing. The large-scale geometric design was developed around a central motif using wonderful rust-reds, yellows, off-whites, blues and turquoise. It was common practice to fade and 'antique' these rugs before supplying the European markets and these colours go particularly well in our climate.

The designs of Samarkand carpets are generally based around three large medallions in line. Owing to the fashion here in the 1930s of chemically fading them, the colours are delightfully washed out. Twenty years ago, most dealers would have dismissed these rugs as having been ruined by this practice. Now, the most reputable dealers will exclaim with excitement that they have a faded Samarkand, that beautiful type of rug so popular in the days of Syrie Maugham. In those days, they were subjected to a fading process so that they could fit into the all-white colour schemes of the period. Today, they are chosen because they are ideal companions to the aged, mellow look of an English country house.

The carpets described here obviously represent just a few of those that have found their way into English houses. They are the types most often seen in the context of English furniture of all sorts and qualities. They are strong in design and so familiar that they have become as English as Palladian architecture. For this reason they have cohesive presence which helps to bind together both new and old.

RUGS, ESPECIALLY FLAT WEAVE like this kilim, look better on Brusels weave than on Wilton carpeting.

131

PART III
COLEFAX & FOWLER TODAY

JOHN FOWLER'S LOVE OF INSTRUCTION AND ENTHUSIASM FOR HIS SUBJECT MADE A huge impression on all those who came into contact with him. He was a man of impeccable taste with an assured eye; to him attention to detail was an intrinsic part of excellence. This is the basis of our inheritance today and without it the firm would not exist in its present form.

After the war Colefax & Fowler consisted of John Fowler and his two or three assistants working on a wide variety of town and country houses. The emphasis was mainly on upholstery, designing curtains, working out colour schemes and paintwork and choosing carpets from within a relatively narrow range. Many of the clients for whom Fowler worked had quantities of furniture of sublime quality. If they wanted something particular they would, in those halcyon days, motor off to country sales or come to London to find it.

Today there is not just one team, but six teams, and the range of fabrics has grown hugely; the variety of carpets, mostly our own designs, has expanded and because furniture is either so expensive or difficult to find clients will often rely on all of us to take a much more positive lead in this respect. In principle, the firm is still as it always was. Fabrics are still dyed to order, but with perhaps not quite the same confidence as the art is not what it was twenty years ago. In addition, an enormous number of trimmings are designed and made, carpets are specially woven to particular colourings and specialist painting is used extensively on every job. George Oakes still runs the painting studio, producing an immense amount of work to support the decorators in the manner that Fowler expected in the past. Tom Parr, who joined the firm to become its second decorator in 1960, has made his own unique contribution. As Chairman of the company, he embarked on a series of brilliant retail enterprises which made available to the general public the best of our wallpapers, fabrics, carpets and accessories, and shops have been opened to sell them. As a decorator, he has completed commissions all over Europe and America.

Stanley Falconer, Imogen Taylor and I, supported by Wendy Nicholls, Vivien Greenock and Roger Banks-Pye, each heading their own teams, work on a variety of commissions. These range from boats to offices, hotels and flats, but most of all it is the houses that inspire us; the memory of John Fowler, a quizzical and eager friend with a mass of observations, accompanies us on every job that comes our way. In decoration, the circumstances as well as tastes change and the rules have to be adapted to meet them; but the standards remain constant. This section of the book looks at a few categories of rooms in which we have completed work and discusses the ideas behind them.

CHAPTER 9

The Changing Role of the Interior Decorator

A MODEL FOR A LIBRARY. THIS entirely new interior, to be built in the Gothic manner out of oak, is to house an important private collection of books and early manuscripts. Two floors of bookstacks are lit by clerestory windows.

THE GROWTH OF INTEREST IN INTERIOR DECORATING OVER THE LAST twenty years has been phenomenal and seems to have inspired a pitch of creative effort beyond all expectations.

As a more frenetic world confronts us daily, we continue to seek our identity through the same stereotype activities of work, home and play. But as life speeds up and the structure of the world around us increasingly intervenes, our interiors assume greater importance as places of refuge and retreat. The incessant noise and scale of the man-made environment is oppressive, and the visual thrust of commercial imagery desensitizing. Those quiet landscapes that so inspired the romantic poets of the early nineteenth century now look better on film: the hills and vales are eroded by suburban sprawl, by the national grid and by an ever-expanding system of roads and human traffic. Setting aside the human misery, even William Blake's 'Satanic mills' suggest a certain scruffy charm which might be more endearing that the sanitized landscape that we may soon be facing.

Each age must find the means to pursue its own ideas and identity and this, at its highest level, becomes art. In the eighteenth century, English gentlemen were inspired by a picturesque dream; familiar with Theocritus and moved by the paintings of Poussin and Claude, they flocked to Italy to find that source of inspiration and to bring back home as many tokens of this spirit as could be acquired. In England they recreated their Arcadia through the parks and gardens in which they set their Palladian houses, temples and statuary. Later, Keats, Coleridge and Wordsworth found their inspiration in nature, as if its secrets were revealed for the very first time. Painters and craftsmen followed in their wake and so fashioned the taste of a whole generation. In the early 1930s there seemed to be the possibility, following social upheaval and artistic revolution, that bourgeois materialism would be swept aside for ever. Preoccupation with possessions and ostentatious display were to be replaced by a set of pure aesthetics, endowed with all the mysticism of truths revealed. The chastity of this abstract grammar was to be for the spiritual benefit of all, rich and poor alike: a Utopia of pristine simplicity set in great parks in which the extended family could work, laugh and play together for all time.

In our age we seem to have chosen the private place, the garden, the home – and particularly the rooms within it – as a metaphor for the world at large, or at least as we would like to see it with 'an eye made quiet by the power of harmony'. This is the stage set of our own making where dreams can be fashioned, the imagination extended and creative expression fulfilled. Here is a realm over which we have complete control as we sit and relax by the fire with family and friends. We drink, share food, gossip, talk of hopes and share ideas; this is the summation of who and what we are.

It is therefore not surprising that fine houses are at such a premium given that the nobility of their architecture offers a wealth of possibilities. In the current passion for antiques it is not just furniture, pictures and rugs that are bought, but everything, right down to the *petits sous* of life, is now pursued to furnish this world of our own creation. Before, the collector of the fine and rare was concerned with his collection: nowadays antiques may be important to those creating interiors but they tend to be subordinate to the decoration. The overall mood takes precedence over the quality of individual items. The right piece is still crucial, but only in that it ideally serves in having the right scale, tone and function. The small things, the incidental details such as the fenders, fire irons, bellpulls, basins and taps, all contribute to the creation of the overall mood, for nothing should be discordant.

For the first time since the early eighteenth and nineteenth centuries, the interior is important once again. The decorator has recovered his position of trust after a lapse of nearly 150 years. Now he is encouraged to orchestrate ideas and produce interiors that are worthy of the tradition that begins with the great Huguenot architect and designer Daniel Marot and threads its way through that list of outstanding men such as Kent, Adam, Borra, Soane, Hope, Papworth and Blore whose works remain a supreme inspiration to us all.

We live in urgent times. People require a more complete service, one that is much more professional and carried out more quickly than in the recent past. No longer are houses built in Arcadian parks to apotheosize a family's name – hugely staffed, largely self-sufficient through their estates, there to serve future generations forever. These days, it is not uncommon for a family to change houses two or three times within the space of one generation. The vagaries of fortune and the speed with which people's lives develop have brought about a wholly new mobility. The decorator feels this urgency more than ever. His new position of trust carries with it further responsibilities. He is in charge, and controls all aspects of interior design from the trimmings of a valance to thermostatic valves.

When Colefax & Fowler first opened for business, it ran as a shop, selling fabrics, papers, carpets and upholstery as well as making up clients' schemes and painting their houses. Occasionally, advice on furniture was sought, but this was unusual. For John Fowler to have been asked to produce any drawing other than what was necessary for a curtain design, the shape of a tassel or a stencil would have been unheard of. Architects, those who understood traditional buildings, produced the drawings for the houses, and whatever constituent parts were required. Fowler would have been speechless if a client had asked him for advice on an electrical plan, kitchen equipment or 'built-in' cupboards. His doodles on scraps of paper showing the spaces between pieces of furniture were often a sufficiently accurate guide to the

THE CREATION OF THIS HALL IN Sudeley Castle is typical of the work undertaken by our architectural studio. The design and detail of the staircase, inspired by the mid-seventeenth-century model at Coleshill, is supposed to look like a later addition, but one that can hold its own in the context of the medieval architecture.

OPPOSITE: AN ELEVATION OF one of the hammer beams for the Gothic library.

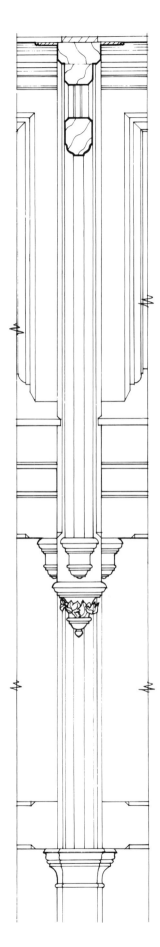

layout of a room, but they were never to any known scale. His detailed instructions, such as for architraves or cornices, were drawn straight on to the walls of the house being worked on and stayed there until the joiner or plasterer had made up whatever was required. Despite much protestation, the painters were sometimes made to paint around such sketches.

The whole approach to decorating then was much more amateur and experimental, but costs at the time allowed for this. If Fowler was not satisfied with a colour, it was 'blotted out', the scaffolding was re-erected and the walls completely repainted – twice, in the case of the Library at Wilton, in Wiltshire. The clients were not happy but they remained silent in the understanding that the effect sought was important and had to be right. Furthermore, they accepted his aesthetic integrity. When it came to upholstery, two or three frames would be made up and partially upholstered so that backs could be adjusted, seats made deeper, arms raised or lowered. The whole process was painstakingly slow, but necessarily so when exact standards were to be achieved. Nowadays, our practice is to copy the best old models that we can find or to use those that Fowler developed years ago.

Today it would be difficult for us at Colefax & Fowler to approach our decorating in such a manner. Not only have costs within the trades risen astronomically, but also clients now expect what they consider to be professional service, and redoing work at their expense is simply not acceptable. Perfection, however, is rarely achieved with such inflexibility. There are two other great changes. First, there has been an appalling diminution of all those craftsmen – the makers of trimmings, the weavers, the dyers, the specialist metal workers – who years ago were waiting in the wings to carry out the most exquisitely exacting work, adding both splendour and authority to all that was done. It is only the cabinet makers, the painters and gilders who appear to have attracted apprentices from the art and trade schools. The fate of the fine upholsterers and curtain makers, of whom only a few skilled ones remain, hangs in the balance. It is like watching a rare species of bird struggling for survival in a changing and hostile environment.

The second great change concerns the architecture, planning, design and detail that goes into creating the interior shell. The architect's recent training has largely been concerned with preparing him for commercial, industrial and public buildings, with the emphasis on management, bylaws, services and technology, and so there has been virtually no role for him to play with regard to private work. His understanding of how clients, with any sort of privilege, wish to live their lives is less than in the past and so a lack of confidence has begun to emerge between all concerned. The decorator has therefore had to expand his knowledge and abilities to make up for this deficit.

Over the last twenty years Colefax & Fowler Associates, the architectural studio, has formed itself into a practice which can restore, design and build, mostly within the traditional idiom, just about any commission that it is offered. The process of attaining such a capability is long and painstaking because the opportunity for training outside the studio, with the exception of a handful of very good traditional architectural practices specializing in this type of work, is nonexistent. Our training has been the volume of town and country houses, dating from the seventeenth to the twentieth centuries, on which we have been able to work. Every detail of plaster, timber, brick and stone is recorded, and when our work demands something beyond our experience, there is a wealth of information at the Soane Museum, the RIBA and Victoria & Albert Museum libraries where designs and details can be studied, recorded and used. The other essential ingredient in a good studio is the enthusiasm with which such an architectural grammar is used. For design work to have vitality and life, the custom of re-using traditional details has got to be imaginative and handled with that spontaneity that only comes with much practice. This pays far greater homage to the past than just a slavish copy.

In the last four or five years, Colefax & Fowler have been offered an increasing number of private commissions that go way beyond anything that the company would have undertaken in the past. One such instance is the design, detailing and fitting out of a large private library to house one of the most important collections of books to have been compiled in our time. Many of the volumes and manuscripts are of a great age and rarity and, in order that they could all be fitted into the space, a gallery had to be included. A design in the Gothic manner was specified in the brief. The process of researching and designing a consistent set of details, from the tiniest Gothic ballflowers, through elaborately carved bosses to the large stone profiles, so that they are all part of the same language, is rewarding. The task of working out how the panelled ends to bookstacks tie in visually with the timber columns, that in turn run into the hammer beams which support the compartmented roof, is highly complex. All these elements are enriched, so that the modelled oak surfaces resemble a Gothic coffer turned inside out. The floor is laid with a carpet designed to mirror the roof's radial pattern and medieval stained glass is set into clerestory windows so that all is bathed in a shifting panoply of tinted light – an echo of the illuminated manuscripts enshrined beneath. The complexity of this type of commission gives some indication of how the decorator's role has been extended.

While we were working on the library, we were asked to submit designs for a folly to be sited within view of a house that we were completing for another client. We were so infused with the Gothic spirit that we designed this little building in the same manner. We did not adopt the early nineteenth-century mood of the library, which owes so much of its inspiration to the work of Edward Blore, but turned to Batty Langley, whose published drawings in the early part of the eighteenth century were amongst the first Gothic Revival designs in England. Our little hexagonal building is developed from one of his proposed fireplaces. Increased in scale, with the addition of elaborately mullioned windows and fitted out with seats and a false bookcase housing a fridge, sink and cabinet above, it is a quiet place for an afternoon's contemplation with refreshment to hand.

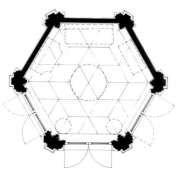

A GOTHIC REVIVAL SUMMER house.

OPPOSITE: AN ELEVATION OF one of the Gothic library bays. Each bay has a niche with a quatrefoil frame for busts of literary worthies. The grammar of these details was inspired by the work of the early nineteenth-century architect Edward Blore.

Another recent commission involved the design, structure and interior decoration of a new house, as well as advising on works of art and the buying of antiques and *objets vertus* – all the small details that lend conviction to that 'lived-in' look. The original house, which the client had intended to refurbish, was a disappointing affair with a wonderful garden landlocked behind the gardens of the surrounding houses. The client, fortunately, recognized the shortcomings of the house as clearly as he appreciated the splendour of the garden, and so down came the house.

It might be supposed that designing a building from scratch would be an easier way of arriving at a series of ideal interiors, as all the architectural compromises are removed. However, this is not the case because, when faced with a blank canvas, all is possible and the options are endless. The owner listed his requirements: the number of reception rooms, bedrooms, bathrooms, dressing rooms and staff accommodation; he also stipulated the optimum size for each. It was when the house turned out to be twice as big as he was prepared to build that the excitement began. The design concept was not, in fact,

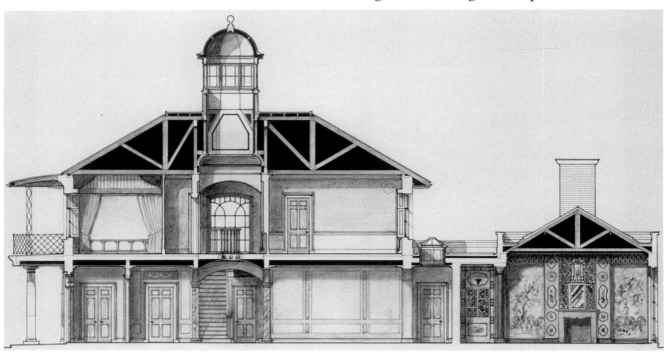

THE FRONT-TO-BACK SECTION of a London villa. The first floor landing and the ground floor are lit by a cupola. At the far end of the house is the Chinese dining room. The hall is wide enough for chairs, side tables, sculpture and paintings and the walls are painted in *trompe l'oeil* to represent panelling.

so difficult to arrive at because the whole area had been developed by one landowner around 1830, with notable architectural continuity. All the neighbouring houses were stuccoed; some Classical, some Gothic Revival, some high and others low. They all had pleasant Regency proportions, and the Classical houses had shallow roofs with deep eaves; the windows were typical with their large panes and fine glazing bars. In the design of the new house we matched many of these details exactly so as not to disrupt the architectural harmony within the area.

The form of the house, however, was quite different from its neighbours. Our site was not in a terrace but in the open, with considerable space all around it, and therefore a villa could be designed.

139

WALL TREATMENT FOR THE Chinese dining room in the London villa. Since there was not enough of the eighteenth-century Chinese wallpaper to cover the walls completely, panelling was designed to make up the difference.

SOME OF THE PANELLING WAS lacquered green and then enriched with gold and silver leaf. Other panels were designed as blind Chinese fretwork with burnished and embossed silver leaf decoration behind. The panelling in this corner conceals a door from the servery. Cantonese plates reflect background light, concealed within the brackets.

COLOURBOARD OF MATERIALS used in the Chinese dining room.

The concept of the villa has a long and noble lineage from the earliest, Colen Campbell's Wilbury Park (1715) and, a little later, Mereworth Castle, to Lord Burlington's Chiswick House and those astylar examples by Sir Robert Taylor with their ingenious and dramatic internal planning. Later they became even more popular, but were beginning to get smaller by the early nineteenth century. This one was still more compact. The idea was to give interior dimension by incorporating some of the architectural devices typical of the Taylor villas. We set a cupola high on the roof through which light could flood into the first floor hall. A tiny circular galleried well was cut into the first floor by which natural light could even reach the ground floor. It is possible, therefore, to stand at the very centre of this building and look up to see the sun tracking round the cupola windows high above.

The ground floor has a long hall running through it, large enough to take side tables, pedestals, statuary and pictures. The decoration of all the rooms is elaborate, and typical is the dining room off the end of the hall. The conception of this room began with the acquisition of things that both the client and I had seen and liked, such as an eighteenth-century hand painted Chinese wallpaper on a pale green ground from a house in Scotland and an early nineteenth-century Mason's ironstone chimney-piece in the Chinese taste from Geoffrey Bennison. A large Chinese glass picture was bought in the sale rooms to go above the chimney-piece. As it was not large enough, we designed an elaborate giltwood cresting in the form of a Chinese pavilion to take a pair of *famille rose* figures, set to survey the feasting guests beneath.

We knew when we bought the Chinese wallpaper that there was not enough to complete the room and so we designed panelling to make up the difference. High double doors into an adjacent room and two other single doors reduced the wall area considerably; we then panelled the chimney-breast and, by adding Chinese red lacquer pilasters, covered up sufficient wall for the paper to fit exactly. The panelling is rich in effect and was devised with pattern on pattern and subtly reflective surfaces for the *famille verte* and Cantonese plates. All the doors and the panelling are lacquered green in the Chinese manner with raised gold decoration. Burnished and embossed silver leaf panels are set behind the Chinese fretwork to reflect the space diffusely so that when candles are lit at night mystery is added to the evenings spent there. Based on a Cantonese frieze, the design of the carpet connects the colours of the wallpaper, the curtains and the fireplace in an Oriental palette of colour.

This sort of commission, following the overall concept right through to the last detail of the most complex decoration, is comparable to other work being undertaken by Colefax & Fowler in both Europe and America and reflects the importance with which interiors are now viewed. To design a house on this scale, with all its details, involves the production of some 300 working drawings besides specifications and trial samples. The logistics are comparable to that of completely designing a large hotel, but here everything has to be generated from within our own architectural studio because there are so few who understand this kind of work. Designs for painted pelmets, floral friezes and carpets then involve the Colefax & Fowler paint studio so that the corporate effort becomes enormously involved. To this must be added the teams of craftsmen on whom we rely heavily to carry out specialist painting, lacquering, gilding, weaving and upholstery.

Work of this scale and complexity has had further repercussions, for in its wake have come commissions of a completely different nature for hotels, shops, offices, aeroplanes and boats. Although hotels and shops can be treated so that they fit all the old precepts of Colefax & Fowler, the others cannot. For even we, who are committed to a style suggesting time-softened gentility in charming, traditional surroundings, cannot imagine it hurtling through the air at 600 miles an hour. We have therefore developed a contemporary design grammar for jobs where it is appropriate: not the brutal aesthetic of industrial expressionism, but one that is more Classical and, we hope, less subject to obsolescence.

AN EIGHTEENTH-CENTURY Chinese glass picture sits on a Masons ironstone chimney-piece in the Chinese taste. The elaborate cresting, in the form of a small pavilion, was designed to give extra height to the composition.

THE ORIGINAL SAMPLE PANEL OF the Chinese fretwork work produced for the client's approval.

CHAPTER 10   Sitting Rooms

OPPOSITE: THIS LONDON drawing room expresses its owners' love of music in a most picturesque way. Its quality undoubtedly resembles that of many of such 1830s rooms in the earliest days of their occupancy.

PERCEIVING THE WAY PEOPLE SEE THEMSELVES IS OFTEN HOW WE begin. Drawing rooms, sitting rooms and libraries, above all other places, are where these conclusions are given greatest expression. The architecture is important in its own right but, in creating interiors within it, adjustments of both a practical and an emotional nature have to be made so that the occupants can live comfortably: it is like choosing cloth and cutting out of it a suit of clothes to fit.

In many homes the range of family interests can be best accommodated by dividing them between two, three or even more reception rooms, setting the formal aspects at one end of the scale against a need for comfort or privacy elsewhere. Imogen Taylor, while working for a client in London, was briefed to develop a plan in which just such a variety of requirements had to be encompassed and given coherence by the decoration. The exercise took place in a large mid nineteenth-century town house with a variety of interesting rooms, the principal one being a generous drawing room with a large bay window adjacent to the fireplace and overlooking the gardens at the back. There is a family passion for music and so an elegant formality has been given to the room's decoration, which conjures up the sort of musical evenings that might have taken place here at the time of its original occupation.

Imogen was fortunate in working for a client who was well used to decorating houses and had a keen interest in buying furniture and pictures and collecting the necessary bits and pieces that give a house warmth. Together they found the Indian cotton festival dhurrie which perfectly fits the room and on which the whole colour scheme is based. Musical instruments dominate. A baby Steinway was lacquered white to lighten its presence; the 1715 Joseph Mahoon spinet was inherited, but the Erard harp and the sundry collection of flutes and horns were mostly acquired later. The mood of this room is in part a result of the client's collection of beautiful things, but there is also a gracious calm in the decoration which exhibits the subtlety of Imogen's talent. Wit and assurance lie behind the choice of the lyre-ended Regency settee, which amusingly echoes musical instrument forms. The pair of silhouettes with the glitter of the Irish *girandole* between them have delightful visual punch, but, above all, the George Romney portrait of a young girl reading a book in the open air is sheer joy. She seems to embody all that is perfect in that most elegant period; moreover, her cream-coloured dress and blue sash give further

143

point to the room's hue.

The skirted table – a patchwork quilt predominately of browns and beiges – matches, with its graphic vigour, the strength of the carpet. The blue of the large sofa and the seats to the pair of painted Directoire chairs establishes, with the background colour of the carpet being echoed again in the curtains, the room's main theme. The curtains attend one fairly conventional window and the very wide bay. In order that they should not overwhelm the room, the dress curtains have been made of raw Indian silk two tones lighter than the ivory-coloured walls. The effect is highlighted by their design and enrichment. Five swags span the bay in alternate sizes, ending in balloon tails finished with a blue and white block linen fringe. The heading consists of a ruched band on which *choux* catch the draperies and bows catch the tails, all made of blue and white striped cotton, cut on the cross. The festoon blinds are in the same striped cotton, with gathered frills bound in blue. A huge window seat is covered in the off-white silk, on which there is a mass of multi-coloured cushions. A pair of armchairs are also in off-white but have red piping which is taken from the red edging of the carpet's medallions. This is a light cool room, for 'posh occasions' as the client expressed it.

In the brief was included, as a contrast, a second, all-purpose, family room, library or working room. Red and green is the theme initiated by the delightful Victorian needlework rug; Colefax &

THE IVORY WHITES IN THE decoration are offset by a beautiful Indian festival dhurrie. The carpet's blue is repeated on the principal sofa, to the left of the fireplace, and carried up into the trimmings and detail of the curtains.

144

drawing room is divided into four distinct seating groups. There is one adjacent to the fireplace, another against the opposite wall and two further seating groups at each end of the room. A basic red and green colour scheme acts as back-up to the splendid Bracquenié printed *toile* which covers the walls.

Fowler's chintz 'Tree Poppy' supports it and is used for the curtains and for a pair of cushions on the green sofa. The bright red walls are strong and enveloping, and everything looks good against them. Most of the woodwork is painted white, except for the principal bookcase which has been dragged in a scruffy old 'lawnmower' green. This piece of furniture hides the television, hi-fi and other equipment that might disrupt the cosiness of the place when not required. The round table in the window is used as a library table or for cards, sometimes for supper, sometimes a general mess. This is the hub of communal family life.

The proportion of our work that is concerned with houses and apartments in cities such as London and New York is higher than ever before. Very few of them are just places of convenience, *pieds-à-terres* to overcome the agony of commuting; more usually they are proper homes, often the most important. The astronomical cost of metropolitan houses and flats is reflected in the attention to detail with which they are designed. Interiors become the focus of much pride and therefore the centre of busy social lives planned with immense care.

When Tom Parr and Wendy Nicholls were asked to decorate a house overlooking Hyde Park, the brief established that entertaining was important. Two interconnecting reception rooms on the first floor and the ground-floor dining room had to accommodate twelve to fourteen people in great comfort. The second objective was the

145

OPPOSITE: IN THIS LONDON drawing room the octagonal table used for books or cards stands in front of a delightful portrait of the young Sir Joseph Banks. The main concern in the decoration was the marriage of the fine English portraits with the collection of French Transitional and Louis XVI furniture.

THE COLOURBOARD FOR THE interconnecting drawing room and library (overleaf). It shows the balance of greens and reds and how the geometric and floral motifs relate to one another.

ABOVE RIGHT: AT THE OTHER end of the drawing room a sofa in green 'Palma Damask' sits under another portrait of Joseph Banks. This scheme is put together with great subtlety. The green glazed Quianlong pot is as striking as the red cushion beyond it. Either side are two more cushions in a rare eighteenth-century German woven silk.

marriage of a most distinguished group of English portraits, principally of Sir Joseph Banks, with a collection of fine eighteenth-century French furniture.

As the building has little architectural merit, with rooms long and narrow in proportion, visual impact had to be achieved by other means. When John Fowler had difficulties with the decoration of the awkward staircase at the Hunting Lodge he overcame the problem by swamping it with a bold pattern. In this case Tom and Wendy's solution is similar, but in grander terms, producing an immensely luxurious and memorable effect.

As the châtelaine of the house is French, it seemed appropriate that the overall flavour given to the decoration of the drawing room should be French. This is achieved in part by the formality of the room's plan and the refinement of the Louis XVI furniture, but most of all by the use of the Bracquenié printed *toile*. This glorious large-scale design of roses and trailing leaves in deep greens, reds and pinks covers the walls, curtains and most of the smaller chairs. It is complemented by other rich materials, particularly the deep green silk damask used on some of the Colefax & Fowler sofas and the larger *fauteuils*. The room's authority is further established by painstaking attention to detail: a two-toned pink and off-white rope edges the upholstered walls, a two-toned green bullion fringe skirts the sofas and an extremely rare eighteenth-century German woven silk of silver and pink rosettes on a striped green ground is used to cover cushions. Plain red silk on other cushions and the backs of certain chairs has also been chosen to echo the red in the *toile*.

The curtains have serpentine-shaped valances finished at the base with a pink linen fringe. The headings are gathered, but each incorporates two goblets with rope knotted at their waists and finished with tassels. For privacy, festoon blinds in natural coloured shantung silk are used beneath the curtains, on the road side of the house. The 'Buxton' carpet is one of our own and has been coloured to tie in with the fabrics. This runs through to the library, which has been conceived as a more masculine extension of the drawing room, while still honouring the same colours and patterns. The library walls are upholstered in a *velours de lin* which has been 'gaufraged' with a stripe. Festoon curtains in a *strié* green silk are reefed to the window heads, green silk damask and the *toile* reappear in the upholstery, and books rather than pictures prevail. It is, however, the *toile's* overall pattern that dominates the whole of this first floor, but not in a way that is disrespectful to the contents. It manages to reconcile the English pictures and the French furniture by the very confidence of its eighteenth-century fantasy – something that would not be possible with two collections of lesser quality.

THE LIBRARY WALLS ARE covered in a green *velours de lin*. The 'Buxton' carpet with its green and red cartouches unites the two adjoining rooms. Here the *toile* and the green 'Palma Damask' reappear on the upholstery. This scheme is a more sombre, masculine variation of the drawing room, but appropriate for a library.

THIS FIRST-FLOOR DRAWING room in Kensington has all the lightness of Regency London. The formal planning of the furniture and the design and detail of the curtains are an exact reflection of the architectural period of this house.

In the second quarter of the nineteenth century London expanded on a colossal scale. It was the time when the spaces between many of the little villages were filled in with elegant stuccoed terraces, crescents and paired villas. These houses have continued to exert a strong appeal on the popular imagination because of their more generous width, the larger size of their windows and their altogether more sunny disposition. When Wendy Nicholls was asked to accompany some clients in search of such a place, they found one built in the early 1830s on a quiet corner in Kensington. It was agreed that the house should be decorated in a manner that reflected the period in which it was built, but that the mood should be kept light and comfortable, making use of the windows on both sides. Because of their attachment to their family home and garden in Somerset, the clients hoped that something of the country could be worked into the decoration of this London house.

Although Wendy decided that the dining room would be the best arena for this *rus in urbe* exercise, the drawing room has a tranquil quality with its large floral needlework carpet. The curtains are Regency in style and have ruched and swagged headings and balloon tails. Made out of a stone-coloured *faille jaspée* silk, they have charming

149

details like the blue-bound rosettes, a reminder of the cockades of revolutionary France.

The furniture plan also conforms more closely to an earlier fashion than is generally found today. A late eighteenth-century settee in a cotton blue and ochre print is placed in the centre of the room opposite the fireplace. Elegant antique tables are within easy reach. A pair of large-scale yellow silk-covered armchairs, which match in colour the painting by Tissot over the chimney-piece, face into the room. A further pair of pale blue buttoned slipper chairs, with deep blue bullion fringed skirts, sit next to the settee. The furniture in the main body of the room has been kept light in weight so that, with the room's dominant windows, pale shadow-striped wallpaper and mophead bay trees, a charming openness prevails. There is a sofa at the other end of this 'L'-shaped room, with two wing chairs either side of a bureau, so that ten can be entertained with ease – the same number as can be accommodated in the dining room below.

Stately homes and houses of grand scale usually have an architectural presence that outweighs any considerations of self-expression. The owners of such buildings are more custodians than masters of what they have. Where the family has lived for generations, established traditions may emerge, with all their liturgic weight, to shape what a decorator can do. Nonetheless, this generally enriches the end result.

Badminton in Gloucestershire, one of the great houses of England, has been the seat of the Dukes of Beaufort for nearly four hundred years. Viewed from the prospect of Worcester Lodge, three miles away, it is indeed impressive as it lies in the landscape with outspread wings, crowned by cupolas and terminated by James Gibbs's pavilions. Over the years there have been many changes: William Kent remodelled the house in 1740 and Sir Jeffry Wyattville reconstructed many of the most important rooms at the time of the Prince Regent. Throughout the eighteenth century England's finest cabinet makers provided furniture, including William Vile, Chippendale and Linnel who created some of the most celebrated Chinoiserie furniture of the time.

When the 11th Duke succeeded to the title he decided that the private rooms once again needed attention. As he put it: 'The basic idea for the house remains the same because we possess fine pieces of furniture and pictures. It needs freshening up, curtains and so on to be replaced. It is a question of striking a happy balance between what has to be done and what can wait. There are always new things required in a large house, such as materials and covers, all of which become quickly worn when there are so many people in a place.' Vivien Greenock, the Colefax & Fowler decorator who undertook this work, found many aspects of the job enlightening. The Duke, who has been connected with the world of fine art for most of his working life, has an immensely assured eye. When it came to rearranging pictures, he not only knew what he wanted but where and how they should be hung and the results could not be bettered. In another respect, working in houses of this size can be a revelation. If a certain piece of furniture – perhaps a lamp or a chair – is needed and the search exhausted in any of the other rooms, one then goes into the attics. Here there is a wealth of accumulated history and furniture of every sort to be dis-

THE YELLOW ROOM, THE Duchess of Beaufort's sitting room. Two doorways have been turned into bookcases, allowing a more intimate arrangement of furniture. The Colefax & Fowler 'Auricula' chintz covers the sofa and armchair.

THE LIBRARY, BADMINTON.
Ancient leather-bound volumes in the William and Mary shelves provide the best possible background. As the Duchess of Beaufort pointed out: 'Books are so much nicer than wallpaper'.

RIGHT: THE BADMINTON library with a games table and a set of cockpen chairs in the Chinese manner by Linnel. The large comfortable sofas are covered in the 'Bailey Rose' chintz – a special favourite.

OVERLEAF: THE BADMINTON library, showing the frieze of family portraits and busts. One of a pair of Canaletto scenes of the house, painted when he visited in 1748, is hung over the books in an impressively irreverent way.

covered without any need to scour the antique shops and salerooms of London. In fact, the Duke does so compulsively; he enjoys the hunt and the discovery.

The Duchess's sitting room is known as the Yellow Room. On the floor is a much worn but glorious Regency neo-Classical Axminster carpet. On the walls above the white painted dado is a Willement flock 'strapwork' paper from the early nineteenth century. This umber on yellow, scuffed and patinated surface has all the depth and richness to serve the pictures well. Two doorways were turned into bookcases so that the room is now entered through one door only (from behind the camera position). This has created a more individual room with a feeling of comfortable enclosure. The yellow hue is repeated in the striped curtains, and the 'Auricula' chintz in autumn tones covers the huge Colefax & Fowler sofa and chair. A pair of small giltwood *bergères* are covered in 'Seaweed' chintz and an old chintz bedspread skirts the table. This scheme works well within the all-pervasive mood of the room: the chintz lightens and informalizes it while preserving its sense of tradition.

The library is the Beauforts' principal private sitting room. With its early eighteenth-century bookcases, recalling the manner of Daniel Marot, it is authoritatively robust in design but personalized by many family possessions, like the two famous Canaletto views of the park hung over the books. The strong Doric entablature, which divides the

books below from the overpanelling against which the early family portraits and busts have been placed, is gloriously collegiate. A giant-scale Oushak carpet has been laid on to coconut matting. The furniture is arranged around two comfortable sofas, covered in the Colefax & Fowler chintz 'Bailey Rose', which are placed symmetrically either side of the fireplace.

The Duchess is particularly fond of this chintz and had chosen it for the Dower House, known as 'The Cottage', which had previously been their home before moving here. They requested that Vivien should make this room like their earlier library, which Colefax had decorated many years before. 'We know by now just how we like our nest to be,' the Duchess explained, 'comfortable, not conscious of design, with books rather than wallpaper.' All this she got in abundance. Besides the 'Bailey Rose', a green wool rep is the predominant fabric. It has been used on the curtains which have been designed to hang from poles with false pelmets, finished with a darker green wool bullion fringe. This wool rep has also been used for odd chairs, cushions and a pair of skirted tables. Enlivening the whole scheme is the coral-coloured linen which ties in with the red in both the chintz and much of the carpet. Supporting the whole decoration is the furniture made for the house, such as the eighteenth-century cockpen chairs by Linnel with their old red morocco leather squabs. There are games tables and a drinks table weighed down under the mass of bottles, and in this atmosphere of generous hospitality there is the fragrance of hyacinths potted in bowls during early summer. The scent of geranium leaves and other sweet and musty smells waft gently in from the adjoining conservatory to mingle with those of ancient leather-bound volumes.

Sandbeck, designed by James Paine in the 1760s, is another house of great importance. Although it had been built by the Earl of Scarbrough's forebear, it had been little used as Lumley Castle, the family's other home, had been central to their lives for many years. When Imogen Taylor was commissioned to work at Sandeck the brief was fairly daunting; she was instructed to be modest with her ideas as the restoration costs of repairing the structure were considerable. This house stands close to the 'Black Country' and two hundred years of industrial grime had played havoc with the porous limestone out of which it was built. It was decided that the house should be redecorated room by room, and the first one to be undertaken was the Ballroom. For years the family had only used the house when attending Doncaster Races nearby, and as they had no need for a ballroom under such circumstances it had been used as a store.

This magnificent Italianate room stands at the very core of the house on the *piano nobile*. Its huge Venetian windows face out at each end, one prospect over the parkland and the other towards the lake. Largely in deference to these Italianate associations, Imogen recommended that the walls be painted sienna – one can almost imagine John Fowler standing at her shoulder nodding his approval. This colour, in

THE BALLROOM, SANDBECK. The former Earls of Scarbrough only opened up this house on the days they attended Doncaster Races. Therefore this ballroom, for which they had no use, became a store. Since the Scarbroughs now use the house as their home, it has been transformed into a marvellous Italianate saloon.

PREVIOUS PAGE: COCONUT matting on the floor was a bold decision in such noble circumstances. It is an acoustic improvement and suits the visual strength of the bookcases.

a much paler form, is carried up into medallions set within the compartmented ceiling. This is painted out in a range of eight whites, warm tones offset by cooler ones. The dress curtains on the outer windows are of a sienna *faille* taffeta with balloon tails and swagged headings. Their concave shape forms an inverse to that of the higher arched ones in the centre. The draw curtains are of off-white taffeta and are Italian-strung.

Off-white is also used to cover the sofas, and to bag the chandelier chain; the sofas are piped and fringed in sienna. The Zeigler carpet was found in the basement, but must have been specially made for the room a hundred years earlier. The walls and curtains look perfect in the context of its colours. The plain and damask blues are cool against the siennas and the orange of the cushions, but all the colours are reflected in the carpet. The English baroque chimney-piece and the magnificent picture frame above underline the Italianate aspect of the decoration that Imogen played up. Most of the furniture is modest but some pieces, like the pair of giltwood console tables, are important; irrespective of quality, this is a room of harmony and memorable beauty.

Sudeley Castle in Gloucestershire combines all that is most romantic in English houses: a rich and occasionally bloody heritage of ancestral intrigues, the drama of medieval towers and turrets and, perhaps most romantic of all, the Gothic thrill of picturesque ruin. In the creation of a revamped private wing for the owners, Stanley Falconer rose to the challenge of a house with strong roots in the past. By carefully marrying together new and old, with an insistence on sympathetic detail, he has blurred the distinctions between ancient and modern. The result is a subtle interior with the kind of sensitivity for the evolution of the country house which is a key to the best of our decoration.

The part of the house in which Lord and Lady Ashcombe chose to have their private quarters was, at that time, being used as a restaurant, with a series of empty rooms above, all in need of repair. Falconer created a new domestic wing which is in every way consistent with the historic flavour of the other parts of the house. This involved building new staircases, putting in chimney-pieces, opening up old windows and creating new doorways. A corner of one room suffered from being rather dark and a glazed door in a Gothic Revival style overcomes this problem, besides giving access to a private garden outside, so necessary when the public have free rein elsewhere. The stencil design on the walls was inspired by a piece of Tudor carving found upstairs and gives an historical weight to the decoration. This awareness of history runs through the decoration.

In the sitting room, which used to house the Castle shop, Falconer has adapted architectural features from elsewhere in the building. The smoke-blackened chimneypiece was copied from an original, now marooned in a ruined part of the house. The cornice was moulded from a Tudor example and the well-worn oak door complements existing early panelling. Sudeley Castle is in many ways an historical pastiche in which subsequent periods pay court to the original Tudor

interiors. A recent example of this are the Georgian 'Gothick' book-cases, which have been designed to look like the handiwork of some nineteenth-century estate carpenter, honouring the decoration's evolution rather than the original style. The coffee table has a piece of antique cloth draped over it; choux catch the cloth at the corners, revealing the velvet underskirt. The furniture stands on a Zeigler carpet, its tomato-coloured field positive in relation to the neutral colours.

At the other end of the architectural scale, cottage interiors can have a special quality all of their own, largely because one is so close to every surface and detail. Handled with sensitivity, their decoration can be enormously enjoyable, as John Fowler demonstrated with the Hunting Lodge.

THE COMFORTABLE SITTING room at Sudeley Castle was created out of the old shop. Many of its architectural features were copied from originals elsewhere in the Castle.

Stanley Falconer acquired Tughill, a sixteenth-century farmhouse set deep in the Cotswolds, some thirteen years ago. Since then he has worked ferociously on a programme of restoration and addition. What is most notable in his handling of the interiors is the systematic way he has studied and understood the building before embarking upon any major changes, so that when they were finally made the work was executed with an authority and scholarship rare amongst architects – let alone decorators. The refinement of authentic detail, as seen in the stonework, his handling of the new plaster, with all its soft arrises, and the wealth of additional joinery, is laudable. In eschewing dramatic decoration, he has created an atmosphere that is both luxurious and sympathetic to the traditions of the place.

The decoration of the sitting room and morning room on the ground floor is permeated by a mood that is as much French as English. Such an approach is not as irrelevant as it may first seem. Waves of Huguenots came to Gloucestershire during the seventeenth and the beginning of the eighteenth centuries to escape religious persecution and left their imprint on much of the rural architecture. In fact, Falconer discovered and revealed an early stone chimney-piece, covered up by later building work, in the morning room which has a definite French flavour. Later, when he was looking for another for the new dining room he was building, he found a chimney-piece that almost matched, but in France. In a way, this house is a token of homage to those industrious French weavers and wool merchants who made the Cotswolds their home.

Having passed through the outer and inner halls, the sitting room

THE MORNING ROOM AT Tughill, Gloucestershire. The choice of pretty country furniture, like the little French bureau which faces out over a quiet corner of the garden, and the use of rustic fabrics are perfectly judged in this context.

RIGHT: THE OTHER END OF THE morning room, with its French provincial open armchairs and big overstuffed sofa. The Kelim rug has a strong primitive quality which tempers the sophistication of the sofa.

is the first room the visitor comes to. It is dominated by a large hearth, with a pair of comfortable chairs either side. An English eighteenth-century rustic wing chair in its original much patinated leather reminds us of the house's harsher origins. This piece faces a refined French *bergère* of similar date in 'gauffraged' velour. An armchair in a faded linen print, an upholstered stool and a corner banquette enable this room to serve as the comfortable nucleus to the house. The mixing of the refined with the modest achieves a level of extraordinary comfort, but in a manner that is both individual and appropriate. The overall nature of the room's muted tones allows colour and pattern, where they exist, to come forth. The china in a corner cabinet, a red decalcomania lamp, a pretty painted cushion and the Staffordshire piebald rabbit all proclaim the joys of rural life.

The morning room is at the very end of the house. Within the mass of thick stone walls, a window seat has been built beneath the mullioned window. The squab and cushions to this seat have been covered in the red and brown 'Strawberry Leaf' cotton print. This design was much loved by Fowler and often used by him in places of similar simplicity. Other seat furniture is overscaled, with a mass of plump down-filled cushions offering generous comfort. However, this sophistication is played down by the materials chosen – Batiks, a plain brown 'Dalmation' linen, country checks and needlework all relate a modest tale. On the floor covering the 'duck's foot' carpet is a kilim rug, the reds and beiges uniting the room's colours in its chevron patterns. This is fundamentally a bookroom and study; there are two Regency black Japanned bookcases, other shelves built into the thickness of the walls and a desk with a charming view over an intimate corner of the garden. This room has all the enveloping appeal that encourages peace and quiet at the end of the day.

Occasionally, people prefer the relaxed atmosphere of a gentler form of decoration, where elements are chosen simply because they please the eye. The colours should be faded and pretty, and antiques of that modest sort favoured by Fowler years ago should take precedence over more serious pieces. Imogen Taylor worked in a Gloucestershire manor house which epitomizes this approach. In fact, she designed the drawing room and had it built on as an extension with the help of Thomas Williams, a most competent builder in those parts. This room is low, as are the other rooms in the house, and the French chimney-piece has been chosen because here its proportions look better than those of its higher English equivalent. The Mauny wallpaper 'Fleurette' was specially printed in two yellows and white to complement the needlework rug with its greeny gold roses on a buff ground. A mixture of French and English japanned furniture, pretty china, *tôle* and a good giltwood looking glass set this easy mood. Yellow and buff chairs tie in with the off-white curtains and the yellow flounces that finish the pelmets. This is a quiet unpretentious palette, but as fresh as cowslips in a summer meadow.

The study walls have been dragged in a warm beige stone colour. The looking glass above another French chimney-piece reflects the niche on the opposite wall which contains a barometer. The beige

A COUNTRY DRAWING ROOM, specially designed and built. A French accent is given to it by the use of a French chimney-piece and the yellow Mauny wallpaper 'Fleurette'. This charming and relaxed room uses a palette of colours inspired by the floral carpet.

THE STUDY IN THE SAME house. Soft muted tones are used, against which the colours of the cushions and the Bessarabian rug positively sing. There is a modest restraint about the decoration of these two rooms which entirely suits the scale of this Cotswold manor house.

tones give life to the reds in the Bessarabian rug and the pondy greens and pinks of the cushions; these rooms express a contentment with life enjoyed in the country.

This inherited Wiltshire rectory is where Roger Banks-Pye has made his weekend home. It is robust in feel and the rooms are lofty, perhaps reflecting the splendid ideals of its first Victorian occupants. The deep and elaborately profiled skirting boards and cornices, in the absence of dados, give emphasis to the weight and height of the drawing room, and it is this aspect of its character that Banks-Pye has played up. The blue shadow stripe wallpaper, which Fowler first encouraged Coles to print, has been used with great purpose. It is, however, the sense of composition in relation to what goes on the walls that is most satisfying. The scale of the looking glass is perfect, but suggests a naughty hedonism in this most moral of abodes. The corner bookcase surmounted by pots, a devotional statue and a picture behind carry the eye up in the most pleasing way. The composition of the glass pictures, pairs of brackets and pots fulfil the same purpose, as do the tall candelabra on the chimney-piece. The decoration is deliberately random: an old leather club chair, a big sofa in a check, nothing mixed and matched about this lot, save the odd cushion. This is just as it should be.

THIS WILTSHIRE RECTORY HAS lofty rooms matching the spiritual aspirations that might be expected of a man of the cloth. The height of the room has been given further emphasis by the use of a shadow-striped wallpaper. The composition of the decorative elements on the walls pursues the same objective.

In Scotland Banks-Pye became involved with the redecoration of a lodge on the river North Esk largely by chance. The client, Janet Ruttenburg, came into Colefax & Fowler to get a chair covered; when she came to collect it ten days later she was so pleased with it that she lingered to discuss ideas on decoration. A shared enthusiasm for checks and blue and white emerged and Banks-Pye found himself with a commission. The object of this house is that it should serve as a comfortable and relaxed holiday home and a base for house parties, shooting and fishing.

The approach to the decoration is essentially modest. In the sitting room the dreadful orange hessian which was on the walls when the Ruttenburgs acquired the house was not stripped off but left. It was painted over with white emulsion and then heavily sandpapered to show tiny flecks of the straw-coloured fibre, warm against the pure white paint. With the clear northern light of the Scottish east coast, the client suggested white for the curtains as well. Their design is simple: plain gathered valances cover the heads of the draw curtains, but the interest lies in their texture and detail. The coarse stitching and the naive forms of Indian crewelwork pattern their surface. They are lined in a modern blue and white check and edged with a natural loopwool

AN IMAGINATIVE USE OF checks. Inspired by the client's collection of American check homespuns, the decoration incorporates them, in small scale, as linings to curtains and cushions and, in large scale, on the upholstered chairs.

AN EMINENTLY SENSIBLE AND attractive way to decorate a house without any stylistic pretensions. The eclectic mixture of furniture has resulted in a room with quite a modern feel.

fringe. It is the checks that become the room's principal theme. For years Janet had collected American check homespuns. Some are eighteenth century, others nineteenth; some are small, rare and framed, but others could be used and were, as, for example, on the eighteenth-century mahogany games chairs. Checks and plaids in different sizes, types and scale have been mixed, but the colour is always blue. Blue is the subsidiary theme and has been used liberally, on the plain linen armchairs, the ragwork rugs from the Dominican Republic, and the Chinese ceramic garden seats.

As Banks-Pye points out, Janet Ruttenburg has a humorous and an irreverent approach to decoration that is reminiscent of Nancy Lancaster. Many of her 'throwaway' decisions are to be much admired. The English games chairs, for instance, are of very fine quality, as is a handsome eighteenth-century gilt console table (not in picture), but the addition of an old milking stool with its 'as found' Dulux gloss displays a courage that more people should have. A pretty, not very old, linen print was found in an Edinburgh antique shop, and Banks-Pye had the idea of using it back to front. As a result, it has a joyful celebratory quality that is reminiscent of a Bonnard lithograph.

When the Ruttenburgs first started using this house they had no pictures, and so Janet, to relieve the blandness of the bare walls, hung up a half-stripped chimney-piece and there it has remained suspended like some architectural trophy. Later, the decoration was finished off with a collection of beautiful Gainsborough etchings and creamware plates hung around it. The space is light and airy, a mirror image of the expansive landscape outside. This room is the product of two creative people working together in harmony; what emerges is a clarity of idea and an excitement that make this a memorable place.

THE MAIN BODY OF THE drawing room. A range of blues are played against warm off-whites. The huge scale of the cerulean blue check gives a graphic quality to the room, which is reinforced in the smaller checks and also in the way the Gainsborough etchings have been hung.

Millden Lodge (one of the oldest lodges in that part of Scotland) is also on the North Esk. On acquiring it, the new owner embarked on a major refit, with Vivien Greenock as the designer, where the traditional mood of the last century prevails. This – the original – sitting room is warm and enveloping in pleasing contrast to the blustery expanse of the bare hills to the south. The colours are rich and mellow, providing a fitting background to the aroma of Douglas Fir logs burning in the hearth and men back from the shoot, downing strong cups of tea amidst heated debate over the change of wind and the covies that got away.

THE SITTING ROOM IN THIS Scottish lodge produces all the feelings of warmth and enclosure that are welcome in such northern climes. The use of a strong tartan on the walls is a bold, but entirely successful, decision. The Scottish Gothic chairs and table are appropriately plain speaking.

The marvellously bold Stuart tartan walls of this sitting room are a miniature reminder of the Scottish Baronial style at Balmoral, only twenty miles to the west, which had the first of such tartan rooms. Here the Bracquenie cotton print is in blue and russet heather tones which match the colours of autumn, when the lodge is in full use. This fabric and the spotted carpet were both found in Paris on a trip with the client. The Scottish Gothic side table and chairs and the dour mahogany games chairs came with the house; these and a scruffy painted wicker chair project exactly the right austerity. The needlework cushion that contains all the room's colours is a delight, as are the wall-mounted cabinets of moths and butterflies. There are other charming oddities, like the beadwork stool, that give this room a delightful homeliness.

CHAPTER 11

Dining Rooms

OPPOSITE: AN INTIMATE
arrangement has been created
at the end of this dining
room. A buttoned banquette
against the wall and four
eighteenth-century English
chairs in the French taste
surround the table. This room
is for evening entertaining
with soft electric light and
candles.

DINING ROOMS ARE PLACES OF CEREMONY AND SOMETIMES
fantasy. The key to their success is that they should look marvellous when in use. In cities in northern Europe and
America, this is generally in the evening, when daylight has gone and
we are able to set the stage with a softer form of our own making.
Artificial light may be appropriate as a background for pictures and
for side or serving tables, but it is only the warm cast of candlelight
that has the movement and life out of which the numenous is born.

Candlelight goes even further than tungsten in being at the red end
of the spectrum, so both have a bearing on the sorts of colours that
look best. If blues or greens are used these colours turn more beige and
may appear muddy. It is the yellows, melons, siennas, reds and
browns – colours which are in themselves warm that look best,
becoming richer and more glowing. Ormolu, gilt and crystal reflect
the fire of candlelight and so these are the materials that we like to use.

In the house overlooking Hyde Park, Tom Parr and Wendy
Nicholls designed a dining room that was specifically for evening use.
This was possible because elsewhere on the same floor they had
created a large sunny luncheon room overlooking the garden with the
mood of a conservatory. This informal room, with its canted and
panelled ceiling and decorated with painted flowers and leaves, provides the balance to the dining room shown here – a tweed suit at this
table would be about as comfortable as a fly in the butter. In fact, there
are two tables: a centre one to seat eight and a smaller end table for six.
This arrangement offers a certain variety of mood since, with only
four or six using the smaller table with its banquette, more intimate
entertaining is also possible.

The decoration takes its lead from a group of fine seventeenth-
century Stuart portraits, including one of Mary of Modena and
another of 'Minette' by Paul Mignard. It was decided that the mellow
tones of these paintings in their original frames needed a rich but passive background for them to look their best. The walls have therefore
been *trompe l'oeil* painted in a manner that brings the 'Free Renaissance'
ornament of Paris in the 1880s to mind: simulated dark auricular parquetry inlay gives emphasis to the *faux* walnut panelling. The curtains
are rich red silk damask with simple fixed French headings held open
by silk rope and tasselled tiebacks; the banquette is in the same
damask. The dining chairs, two quite different sets, underline the in-
dependence of the two table groups. The higher, rather proper,

167

IN THE SAME DINING ROOM THE principal table has subdued lighting, which emphasizes the richness of the silk damask curtains. The seventeenth-century portrait hangs against a background of simulated inlaid walnut panelling.

English mid eighteenth-century style chairs for the centre table are upholstered in a simulated needlework print of catalpas in flower, on linen. The four English chairs in the French taste are in a pale green cut-silk velvet which matches the leaves of the catalpa flowers to establish just the hint of a visual link. Altogether this is a refined and sophisticated form of decoration that answers the brief exactly.

It was in response to her client's request for the infusion of a country spirit that Wendy Nicholls designed the dining room for the corner Kensington house. A set of ten gloriously painted Portuguese chairs gave birth to the idea for the decoration. In form, these match George I models, but this similarity is not uncommon in Portuguese eighteenth-century furniture due to the close trade links and an unbroken political alliance between the two countries. These chairs are extremely pretty in their decoration; each baluster splat is painted with different flowers in a form of painted enrichment that so impressed John Fowler when he visited Cintra in the 1950s. They were bought through Jack Wilson, an antique dealer whose taste much paralleled Fowler's own. Since before the war, he was one of the very few sources from whom this sort of furniture could be acquired, so it seems fitting that they should end up with a Colefax & Fowler client.

Sienna glaze-painted walls, finished with a flat varnish, always look good with pale stone or stuccoed architecture. Here the colour is a perfect background for the chairs and the Besler botanical prints. Plants and flowers continue to influence the choice of things, for example, the Colefax 'Strawberries' carpet and a collection of wonderful Chelsea botanical plates and dishes, five of which in a leaf form can be seen on the mantlepiece. The Regency curtains have been made in a green and white ticking, lined with green Shantung silk. The valances are swagged and thrown over the poles in a design that is quite different in effect from the drawing room upstairs, but equally appropriate in the context of the architecture. At night the colour of the walls becomes deeper, richer and more enveloping; during the day, with its blooms and fruit, the room becomes a celebration of summer, a perpetual harvest festival.

THE SWAGGED NEO-CLASSICAL curtains in a green striped fabric have been designed to match the period of the house.

THE BOTANICAL THEME OF THE room continues with the Brussels weave 'Strawberries' carpet.

RIGHT: THIS LONDON DINING room is a celebration of summer. The decoration's botanical theme started with the painted eighteenth-century Portuguese chairs, which were then given support by the early Besler prints and the Chelsea china. Even the marble chimney-piece was chosen because of its floral enrichment.

Architecture has the potential to inspire, and can often determine the whole mood of a dining room, but possessions, pictures and furniture are just as important. Our way of using dining rooms has been less influenced by changing social patterns than that of any other room in the home. We still sit around the same sized tables in the same numbers, using chairs of the same height and proportion; the food and the table conversation represent the only appreciable differences. As a consequence, many of Colefax & Fowler's rooms have all the substance of traditional values that have remained unbroken since the time of their apparent conception. The two dining rooms illustrated here are typical in that they have a comfortable early nineteenth-century feel about them – a balance between pictures, colours and furniture which is both harmonious and distinguished.

When he designed the dining room in a fine early nineteenth-century white stuccoed house that he redecorated in Belgravia, Stanley Falconer chose to make the decoration pay its respects to the architecture. Colefax & Fowler's 'Clover Leaf' carpet, inspired by stone paving, covers the floor as a background; over this a neo-Classical Pontramoli needlework carpet has been laid. Stripes have been painted on to the walls and a two-toned rope runs under the cornice and above the dado rail. The curtains have been made up in the 'Tree Poppy'

THE MAUNY WALLPAPER, THE pair of pictures and the chandelier give a French caste to this Regency dining room. The swagged neo-Classical curtains in deep yellow taffeta repeat the idea in the paper border.

THIS DINING ROOM TAKES ITS cue from the early nineteenth-century architecture. The decoration has strong Regency associations, but the 'Tree Poppy' chintz has been worked into the scheme to soften this severe Classicism.

chintz and the draperies which hang over a pole in a neo-Classical manner are finished with a two-tone block linen fringe. The result is a fine room recalling all the elegance of Regency life.

Recently Imogen Taylor designed this pretty yellow London dining room, a fanciful, predominantly Regency room, to which she has added a 'dash of French' through the use of a Mauny wallpaper. This paper is in imitation of gathered yellow taffeta hung from a pole which has then been swagged with fabric, tassels and white rose garlands. The curtains, which are made out of a deep yellow taffeta, repeat the idea of the paper border, but on a larger scale. Black and yellow always look good together, and so the dwarf cupboard, the black curtain pole and the set of fine Regency chairs all relate to one another in a most pleasing way.

Dining rooms in cottages and smaller country houses can be more informal, especially as they come into their own at weekends when guests and friends have left the pressures of work behind them. Stanley Falconer designed and added this dining room, as part of a new wing, to his Gloucestershire cottage. This room has all the mass and exact detail of the original structure; it is as if it has been 'felt' into existence rather than brought about by drawings and specifications. The artisans of the past erected buildings in this way and that is the secret behind the pleasure they give. The floor is of broad elm boards, used for paupers' coffins and cottage floors; it is a hard-wearing timber with delightfully vigorous figuring. The walls are glaze painted in the same honey colour as the rest of the ground floor, giving continuity throughout.

OPPOSITE: THE SOFT YELLOW tones of these dining room walls suit not only the old tan leather of the chairs but also the modest architecture. The whole scheme is invigorated by the glorious Zeigler carpet.

THE VIEW THROUGH INTO THE dining room from the recently completed kitchen.

LEFT: THE BUFFET HAS BEEN lined in a check *toile*, an ideal background for the display of the French faience. All the furniture in this room is Continental.

OVERLEAF: THE DECORATION OF this Wiltshire rectory dining room is based on the screen, which was found in the Brook Street basement.

At the end of the room stands a stone chimney-piece found in France, the pair of the one in the morning room. Falconer has created a French mood in this room by his liberal use of Continental furniture, particularly the fruitwood dining table and eighteenth-century *fauteuils*. The mellow tones are offset by a rich Zeigler carpet on the floor, the Delft garniture on the chimney-piece and another delightful display at the opposite end of the room charmingly composed in a buffet that has been lined in a French check *toile*. With the two Carolean silver sconces on the chimney-breast, the wall lantern and the pairs of candlesticks on the side and dining tables, at night this room has a magic to be remembered.

Roger Banks-Pye converted the Rectory's old Victorian kitchen into a dining room. With a new working kitchen adjacent, meals can be prepared with no break in the easy flow of conversation – the height of weekend informality. This room has been put together with relentless determination. The old cast iron range, and its mantle, the dresser, the walls and every available surface have been overlaid with blue and white china of every conceivable type. Some of it is English willow pattern or Delft; other pieces are from China and Morocco; some are old; others new. The whole idea for the room began with the discovery in the basement at Brook Street of an apparently unwanted screen of *trompe l'oeil* blue and white china on a yellow ground that had been painted by George Oakes in the 1960s. Banks-Pye bought it cheaply – perhaps, on reflection, not so cheaply when one considers

the subsequent unbridled course of his imagination. Its colour scheme encouraged him to use blue and white on everything, with yellow walls as a background. The curtains were made in a white fabric on to which blue and white napkins were sewn, in checkerboard fashion. Blue and white machine-made needlework covers the seats to the old Scottish chairs, and one of a variety of blue and white cloths, in this case an Italian bedspread, covers the table. The result is a witty and an amusing room where historicism has given way to something that is more spontaneous. The profusion of china and other bric-à-brac is the result of browsing in the shops of country antique dealers, a habit which is in itself a pleasant relief from the mighty industry that dominates the art world of London's West End.

PREVIOUS PAGE: THE OLD kitchen dresser crammed with blue and white.

THE BLUE AND WHITE CHECK dusters sewn on to the simple white cotton curtains are extraordinarily effective – imposing, yet entirely appropriate to the origins of the place.

BLUE AND WHITE CHECKS abound, the screen is covered in the check which lines the adjacent drawing room curtains, the chairs are slip-covered in dust sheets, and even alternate squares of the rush matting have been painted blue in chequerboard fashion.

A COMPOSITION OF JANET Ruttenburg lithographs. Yellow country chairs against yellow walls, with the odd dash of blue and white, stir memories of Monet's house at Giverny.

The dining room of the Ruttenburgs' Scottish lodge has the same sort of colour scheme as Banks-Pye's own in Wiltshire. This is not, as it might seem, the simple transplantation of a good idea from one side of Britain to the other. Janet Ruttenburg's collection of old document pieces of blue and white check homespun and her expressed love for the atmosphere of Claude Monet's house at Giverny, just south of Paris, were other factors. The parlour of Monet's house is a mass of provincial blue and white checks and yellow-painted country furniture seen against yellow walls. It is easy to imagine how Banks-Pye responded to Janet's taste; it was a case of pure telepathy.

There are two dining tables in the room; one is set in a large bay window, to which yellow-painted ladderback chairs made locally are drawn up; the second appears in the photograph. Janet was so delighted by the effect of this room that she spray-painted her mahogany table yellow in a mood of celebration. The square-patterned rush matting was also painted with alternate squares in blue. Everyone was then encouraged to stamp around on it to scuff it up and patinate the finish. The chairs are slip-covered in dust sheets and the four-fold screen is covered in fabric that matches the lining of the drawing room curtains. Plates and pictures have been hung with great individual assurance, particularly the asymmetrical group of Janet's own lithographs.

177

Stanley Falconer's decoration of this newly constructed dining room within an old wing of Sudeley Castle has exactly the right character. This is due partly to the choice of elements within the room, but more to their scale and disposition. The over-mantle, which was discovered in the attic, was covered in thick brown varnish and looked thoroughly 'reproduction'; now that it has been stripped, bleached and waxed, it has a quality that tells of use through the centuries. The lower section of the chimney-piece was made to match and a pair of crudely carved figures act as jambs. It is, however, the composition of the Charles II Tudor rose wall sconces and the other plates and beakers surmounted by the table carpet that create the appropriate effect.

The walls have been glaze painted a brown colour to suggest great age. On the floor, over matting, a huge-scaled Zeigler carpet has been laid. Perfect for architecture of this weight, it has allowed Falconer to use festooned curtains of matching scale. These curtains are made from a printed linen in faded colours, and finished at their bases with a three-toned wool bullion fringe that picks up the colours in the carpet. A pair of wing chairs in the same linen add visual substance and variety to the group of mahogany dining room furniture. The whole *mis-en-scène* is crowned by an exotic seventeenth-century Portuguese chandelier.

THE DINING ROOM, SUDELEY Castle. The colour of the glaze painted walls suggests great age and tones in perfectly with the huge-scaled Zeigler carpet.

'THE COTTAGE' DINING ROOM, decorated for the Somersets. The bold red lacquer walls make the most of the cornice, the profiles of the overdoors and the pedimented Palladian chimney-piece.

ABOVE RIGHT: THE REGENCY balloon-backed chairs at Badminton slip-covered in white with the Duke of Beaufort's stencilled monogram.

A number of years ago, when Tom Parr decorated 'The Cottage' at Badminton for the Somersets, he produced a delightfully bold red and white dining room. Since they had wonderful family pictures by Wootten of horses and grooms, very stylized and rather wooden like so many mid eighteenth-century conversation pieces, Parr felt that this red would be an excellent background for them. The architecture of the room also benefits from the strength of the colour scheme. The cornice, which is almost too heavy for a room of this height, has been well and truly put in its place, and the entablature over the door, as well as the weighty pedimented Palladian chimney-piece, are also improved by the contrast. At the time the Somersets had four young children and had requested a practical dining room. The red glazed paintwork could certainly withstand the scuffs and finger marks as well as any surface, and it was decided to treat the chairs in an equally practical manner. Rather than restore the morocco leather of these good balloon-backed Regency chairs, it was decided to give them slip-covers in white linen which could be taken off and put into the wash along with the tablecloths and napkins. Visually, they make a perfect contribution to the colour scheme. To add distinction, David Somerset's initials were embroidered on to the backs of the chairs in a monogram which reads 'SID' – causing some amusement.

When David Somerset succeeded to the Dukedom and the family moved into Badminton, the dining chairs, amongst many other things, went too. The covers, however, had been laundered out of existence; they were remade in white union cloth but this time with the monogram stencilled on. Vivien Greenock's brief, as for the rest of the house, was to redecorate the dining room to look as if it had not been touched. The ceilings and the dado were accordingly painted an

aged, greyed white. Most important to this room are the three pairs of curtains that Vivien designed. They are made up in a specially woven all-wool tammy stripe, the scale and colour of which act as a link between the walls and the carpet. The flock wallpaper of a strapwork pattern was designed and supplied by Thomas Willement early in the last century. It provides the most perfect background to the room in the subtle homage it pays to the collection of sixteenth and early seventeeth-century family portraits: the design of the paper matches the damascene patterns in Sir Charles Somerset's armour in the painting by George Gowers. The carpet, a massive Oushak, is coloured in reds, greeny gold and a little blue. The greeny gold is echoed in the background of the wallpaper and is picked up by the curtains, which have swagged pelmets with tails and are finished with a wool bullion fringe, rope and tassels in off-white, red and brown.

OPPOSITE AND BELOW: THE family dining room, Badminton. The dado, architraves and ceiling were all painted in an aged off-white to tone in with the background of the early nineteenth-century strapwork design wallpaper supplied by Thomas Willement.

RIGHT: IN TONE, SCALE AND density of detail, the curtains are a perfect match for the walls, bookcases and the giant Oushak carpet.

Tom Parr designed a dining room in a glorious Directoire house that sits on the edge of Lake Geneva. The house started life as a grand but tiny fishing pavilion and was unusable until permission was recently granted to extend it. Seen in daytime the greyed off-whites and pale greens of this dining room have all the subtlety of untouched eighteenth-century paintwork. The walls' large-scale serpentine tree forms reflect those that surround the house on three sides; this is the Drottninghölm wallpaper, again painted by George Oakes. Round an English Regency table stand six Regency armchairs, in their original black paint, lightly poised in the room with their arms miming the painted branches on the walls. The curtains are made from the simplest of off-white linens bound in green, and the passive pattern of a large Ferahan carpet covers the floor. On summer evenings light reflected off the water throws its dappled patterns into the room, and the eggwhite glaze on the painted leaves shimmers from within the shadows. This is a tranquil place where time stands still and the presence of nature is felt all around.

When Gustave Leven wanted to build a new house on the Riviera it was to the typical Palladian villa of English Classical architecture that he turned to realize his dream. Alan Gore, with John Fowler advising, was responsible for the architecture of this house and Tom Parr created the interiors. The dining room is cool with its lofty spaciousness and marble floor. The walls are glaze painted to a soft flat sienna colour. Although it was conceived as a print room, drawings

ALTHOUGH THE HOUSE SITS ON the edge of Lake Geneva and the painted wall decoration originates from Drottninghölm Castle, Sweden, this dining room has a decidedly English air. There is an ease about its decoration which comes only with the confidence of much experience.

have been used instead. Eighty-two of these have been drawn in the manner of engravings by the artist Hugh Robson, and stuck to the walls in formal compositions with attendant borders and swags.

The room's contents are a balance of refined Louis XVI furniture and other objects of sumptuous presence. The great baroque Chippendale pier glass came from Blenheim and is perfectly placed to reflect the chandelier's candlelight at night. The soft green curtains are Classical in style: the swagged valances have tails and fringes, and there are scalloped overdraperies, scarves in a paler, sharper green silk, all held at the corners by goblets. Behind the whole conception is the guiding spirit of Palladio, the first of the Renaissance architects to attempt, from his imagination, a serious reconstruction of the form of Roman villas, which only years later was proved to be accurate. The appeal of these villas has never ceased to play on the imagination and few rooms could better stand for the purity of this Classical idea.

A COOL DINING ROOM CREATED as a refuge from long, hot summer days on the Riviera. Great neo–Classical draperies help to filter the light and an important Chippendale looking glass reflects the magic of the chandelier.

CHAPTER 12 Bedrooms

OPPOSITE: THIS BEDROOM AT Badminton, which had been used by the previous Duchess of Beaufort, has a sublime Palladian glamour. The Ionic screen harks back to bed alcoves when such rooms were used for reception. The furniture is French, as is the style of the bed's corona in a simplified form. The panelling and the colours of the fabrics have been kept light so that the room glows in the morning sunshine.

RIGHT: IN THIS FEMININE bedroom ethereal white silk taffeta curtains and bed drapes are set against a background of walls upholstered in pink and white stripes. A floral carpet and various chintzes bring a country feeling to the room.

BELOW: THE SERPENTINE LINE of the valances has been given emphasis by a red harlequin trimming, set between the curtain fabric and the fringe. It is also used down the leading edges and at the base of the curtains.

A BEDROOM IS THE MOST PERSONAL ROOM IN THE HOUSE. IT IS THE place where all our private fantasies may be expressed, where life's mementoes are collected – photographs of family and friends, letters and tokens of childhood. Historically, beds have always occupied a place of great importance, understandable considering that we are born in them, like to believe that we were conceived in them, and presumably hope to end our days in them.

As pieces of furniture, beds can be very elaborate and have encouraged much invention in their time. As their presence is so dominant, the rooms in which they stand are often designed as an extension to them. Moreover, their influence is also felt in the decoration of dressing rooms and the bathrooms, binding the whole suite of rooms together in a visual unity.

For the third floor in the Kensington corner house, the clients' brief to Wendy Nicholls was to create a feminine bedroom with the decoration continuing through to an adjacent bathroom and dressing room. They wanted these rooms to be light and sweet, complementing Shannon's painting of Lady Diana Cooper in her wedding dress. The walls are upholstered in a pink and white striped silk taffeta, finished under the cornice and above the skirting with a red picot braid. The drapes to the four-poster bed and the curtains are of white silk taffeta. The valances are finished with a natural-coloured linen fringe and a dyed red harlequin braid emphasizing their serpentine line. The carpet is the old Colefax design 'Bowood' woven with a cut-pile finish. The 'Rose Sprig' chintz used on the eighteenth-century window seat at the end of the bed and on the large armchair with its run-up stool bring into the room that touch of country the clients particularly wanted. The rich paintwork of the late eighteenth-century tester frame with its supporting mahogany posts, the line of the Georgian painted elbow chair, the *tôle* tray table and the exquisite form of the eighteenth-century looking glass give the room a visual strength and a definition that is desirable when such a profusion of sweet colours used.

The light spacious bathroom has the same 'Bowood' carpet running through from the bedroom and all the paintwork is white. The pink has been introduced by way of a small-patterned Mauny wallpaper, specially coloured for the room, and curtains of a pin-striped taffeta. The detail of tiny pink and red rosettes in the curtains' French headings echoes the motifs in the wallpaper. Plenty of mirror adds to the illusion of space in this bathroom, with its charming views over the luxuriant gardens behind.

LADY DIANA COOPER IN HER wedding dress by J.J. Shannon. The decoration of the bedroom was planned around this charming painting.

ABOVE: A DYED RED BRAID edges the upholstered pink and white striped taffeta walls.

LEFT: PINK AND WHITE continue into the master bedroom. The Mauny wallpaper was specially printed to match the pink of the bedroom's striped taffeta. A comfortable chair and a useful table help to furnish the room.

A FRENCH-STYLE BED WHICH IS set sideways to a wall provides the answer when space is tight; it can also be used as a sofa. The pretty green bud motif wallpaper picks up the green in the Colefax 'Climbing Geranium' chintz.

COLOURBOARD FOR THE bedroom shown overleaf, with 'Climbing Geranium' chintz and the 'Lyme Park' paper and border.

OVERLEAF: THE BEDROOM HAS been designed as a sitting room complete with working fire, upholstery, bookcase and a desk. The *en suite* bathroom continues the theme.

At the top of the house are two children's rooms and their bathroom. The daughter insisted on a draped bed but the space was really tight. Wendy has therefore used a Louis XVI-style bed, picked out in colours to tie in with the fabrics, and the drapes are held back by cloakpins at each end. During the day the bed doubles as a sofa. 'Lyme Park', a small bud and leaf motif paper, has been applied to the walls and, as this is an attic room and correctly there are no cornices, a patterned paper border finishes the walls at the junction with the ceiling. The 'Climbing Geranium' chintz in a mauve and green colourway has been used for the curtains, the bed and its draperies, which are lined with a printed *voile* of the same colourway. Pretty creamware botanical plates have been hung on the walls adding delightful spots of colour.

In Belgravia, Stanley Falconer decorated a spare bedroom and an attached bathroom in the manner of a comfortable country sitting room – the approach that Nancy Lancaster pioneered so impressively in the 1930s. These rooms have working fires, carpets, rugs, comfortable chairs, bookcases, a desk, lamps to read by and a variety of things decorating the walls. The bedroom walls have been painted with *faux* panelling, the stiles and rails blue and the panels off-white. An off-white self-patterned carpet covers the floor with a needlework rug on top of it. A delightful French *toile* printed with an eighteenth-century design provides the key to the decoration. This fabric, with its sprigs of blue and red flowers, has been used on the bedhead, a large comfortable armchair next to the fire and the curtains. These are simple, but elegant, and have valances with pencil-pleated headings bound at the top and base. The curtains themselves are also bound and break on the floor. An interpretation of the same sprig pattern is used as a painted wall decoration in the bathroom, so that the two rooms are pleasantly unified. A little check fabric on a small settee at the foot the bed and a variety of cushions introduce a touch of informality into the scheme.

The conventional arrangement of a shared bedroom, bathroom and dressing room is not always the most harmonious solution for busy working couples. A suite of two bedrooms, a bathroom and a dressing room can often work better, particularly when one has the pressure of a disruptive schedule or is perhaps a restless sleeper. It can also be a convenient way for two people to share a life without being in uncomfortably close proximity. When Tom Parr found his exquisite *casella* in the south of France, built by Robert Streitz in the early 1960s, he chose this configuration. The master bedroom is a good size, and has blue fabric covering the walls, with Colefax & Fowler's 'Tatton Park' carpet on the floor. The delightful chintz 'Plumbago Bouquet' has been used on much of the upholstery as well as on curtains which have French-headed valances. The furniture, which includes a French painted wing chair, a *bureau plat* and a handsome honey-coloured English clothes press, sets a masculine stamp on the room.

IN SPITE OF THE CHINTZ, THIS bedroom is without doubt a masculine room. The large English clothes press and the bureau with its wing chair manage to convey this message. With the chair and its run-up stool by the window and the dog's bed in the foreground, there could be no better place for an afternoon siesta.

The second room is a small single bedroom with spare, almost academic, overtones; it could well suit a Regency archaeologist with studies of ancient Rome in mind. One feels that even the furniture has been chosen for the trip. 'Passion Flower' chintz is used on the curtains and walls, but the carpet is the same as in the master bedroom. The nineteenth-century iron bedstead was found in the house, its base, mattress and neo-Classical bolsters covered in a brown fabric which picks up a colour in the chintz.

The master bathroom which connects the two bedrooms is big, and comfortable enough for two to share. Its design is an interplay between the cool white marble, the mellow fruitwood and the small blue and white woven check above the marble dado. The bath occupies the best possible position and in it one can soak while contemplating the deep blue sky of southern France and the olive trees beneath it.

THE MASTER BATHROOM HAS cool white marble on the floor and dado, but the walnut gives the room an appealing warmth.

THE GUEST ROOM BEYOND THE bathroom has strong Regency overtones set against a rich background of the nineteenth-century 'Passion Flower' chintz.

In the villa on Lake Geneva, where Tom Parr designed the dining room illustrated on page 182, he also completed a master bedroom with a two-level bathroom and dressing room. Conceived as a pure English country house bedroom, it has an eighteenth-century four-poster bed (in fact, it is Scottish) typical of many in grander English houses. Here it looks completely at ease in this fine high room with its neo-Classical arched window, richly prepared walls and dado panelling. The paper, 'Les Tulipes' from Mauny, is a French eighteenth-century design in the most subtle greens, yellows and golds running through to deep burnt orange; the scale of the design is perfect. The bed's treatment is superb in its severity which effectively plays up to the extravagance of the window's Regency curtain design; green silk taffeta finished with two-tone block silk trimmings has been used on both. The window treatment is inspired. The Italian-strung curtains are finished down their leading edge and base with a tiny two-toned silk fan edging. The over-draperies in the same silk taffeta are caught in the centre by a bow and swagged to further bows on the extremities, from which hang tails finished in the block silk fringe. Between the draperies and the window's arched head, the silk has been pleated and gives emphasis to the swags. The settee in the window is in the French taste, and a fine English work table stands in the foreground. All the furniture is of excellent quality, as indeed are the

THIS BEDROOM, LIKE THE dining room in the same house, has a predominantly English mood suggested by the bed, the Regency window treatment and some of the furniture. The wallpaper, a beautiful Mauny design of tulips, ties in perfectly with the green silk taffeta.

eighteenth-century Chinese glass pictures on the wall. The Colefax &
Fowler 'Medallion' carpet, which was coloured for the room, runs
through into the bathroom and dressing room.

The bathroom is galleried, with the dressing room upstairs and the
bath set into a recess below. There is a shower on one side and lavatory on the other. A dressing table has been positioned beneath the
window to the left, with a basin balancing the plan on the opposite
side of the room. The walls have been upholstered in a small-patterned fabric and the room luxuriously furnished with an amusing and
interesting mixture of pictures, lamps and furniture.

A DETAIL OF THE BED'S
valance and draperies. Green
silk taffeta finished with block
silk trimmings in ecru and
yellow.

THE MASTER BATHROOM AT ITS
most theatrical. The bath,
shower and lavatory are on
the lower level and there is a
properly furnished dressing
room above.

When it came to the organization of the Rectory's bedrooms
Roger Banks-Pye took a leaf out of John Fowler's book at the Hunting
Lodge; as guests should be made to feel pampered and appreciated,
they should be awarded the most congenial bedrooms. Therefore
Banks-Pye's own, more spartan, abode is tucked right up into the
steep eaves of this building's slightly ecclesiastical profile. A small
Dutch parquetry bed has been placed next to the gable window with
its distant views across the White Horse Downs. His predilection for
blue and white seems to have followed him up here as well. The bedspread is a patchwork of dusters, teacloths and any other scrounged
fragments that could add to its Beatrix Potter quality. The single curtain is made from very fine blue and white unlined striped sheeting,

which can be quite simply hooked over a cloakpin during the day. A simple pinoleum blind that filters the light has been fixed to the window head, behind the curtain. Other furniture, including a Dutch parquetry elbow chair and a Charles X tripod table, has been chosen to complement the bed. The restraint of the walls' white paintwork and the simplicity of the striped dhurrie on the floor underline the discipline of the room's design.

On the floor below, the Rectory's principal bedroom has been set aside for weekend guests. The immediate impression is one of civilized generosity: a large comfortable room filled with family pictures, photographs and drawings. A big double bed, at a sensible height, dominates the room and there are tables for books and flowers, stools for breakfast trays and just about everything a guest could ask for. The colour scheme – a delightful balance of blue, white and pink used in a variety of patterns of different scale – is set by the rich pink ground of an unusual Turkey carpet. The Colefax & Fowler chintz 'Brompton Stock' in greens, pinks and greys was chosen because it picks up the pink of the carpet and has just the right country associations. The Italian-strung curtains have simple gathered headings bound in blue, but their leading edges have been scalloped, pinked and frilled. With the addition of the blue chintz underfrill, a glorious effect is produced that would surely have had the old rector covering his eyes in disapproval. A small pink cotton print has been used on the blind, and the wallpaper is another small design, blue on a pinky cream ground that looks as if it has been tinted by the carpet's reflection. Blue and white china, the blue fabric screen and the bold pattern of the Portuguese bedspread impose a visual order on the whole scheme.

ABOVE LEFT: A SMALL SINGLE attic bedroom. A provincial Dutch bed and chair, with the Biedermeier tripod table in between, makes a charming group. With its blue and white patchwork quilt, the bed is reminiscent of some half-remembered nursery book illustration.

ABOVE: THE PRINCIPAL SPARE room, on the other hand, is very grown-up, embodying all the qualities of comfort. It gives the impression of having been in existence for a very long time and having evolved quite naturally – a mark of the best decoration.

194

As in so many rustic buildings, the bedroom floor of Falconer's Gloucestershire cottage has been squeezed in under the roof. The original windows and eaves, being extremely low, posed some testing problems in the decoration of these rooms. In one bedroom these difficulties have been ingeniously overcome with a tester of Falconer's own design and what might have been a claustrophobic experience has been turned into something rather luxurious. The bed hangings, which are fixed to the eaves, are in the form of a gathered pelmet, contrast-bound at their head and base. The bed's dress curtains, which are held back by cloakpins, are in the same 'Geranium Moiré' chintz as the pelmet. Inside, a gathered chintz lining lightens the effect. A similar pelmet of charming cottage-like proportions is used to decorate the head of the window, and shutters have been installed to keep out the morning light. A wardrobe has been made out of a painted Gothic Revival pelmet from which hang curtains in the same chintz – a most amusing invention. The strong geometric pattern of the nineteenth-century patchwork quilt is a perfect match for the vigour of the dark blue 'Roses and Ribbons' carpet. A pretty off-white side chair in the manner of the great Directoire chair maker Georges Jacob keeps the mood of the room light. The walls are washed in pink and edged in a red braid. The beams have been painted white – a pleasant relief from that nineteenth-century practice of staining them all black.

THIS HALF–TESTER BED cleverly overcomes the problems of steep eaves. The 'Roses and Ribbons' carpet and the painted furniture are firmly in the Fowler tradition.

A SMALL BATHROOM UNDER cottage eaves given memorable presence by its slate-topped vanitory unit and commode chair.

The adjoining bathroom has the 'Sudbury Park' wallpaper, its border giving pleasing emphasis to all the cottage geometry. Small naive patterns are often found in cottage interiors like these and form the ideal background. The mahogany commode chair not only hides the lavatory but gives the bathroom a more comfortable, less utilitarian, feeling. The vanitory unit, with its black slate top and old-fashioned brass taps, suggests that all has been comfortable in this house for a very long time.

Falconer decorated many bedrooms in the newly converted wing at Sudeley Castle, but perhaps none with more subtlety than a small spare bedroom now known as the 'leather dressing room'. The idea behind the decoration began with the discovery of some eighteenth-century Portuguese leather wall-covering in one of the upstairs rooms in the castle. By chance, more was discovered in another house on the estate and so, brittle and black with age, this leather was collected together, painstakingly cleaned with a spirit solvent and an eraser, patched, fed and polished before being applied to these walls. Now this stamped, gilded and painted surface makes as fine a room as can be found, totally appropriate to its castle setting.

The key to its success lies in the support given by the decoration. The dado, cornice, frieze and architraves have all been stippled in a dark brown colour that is weighty, aged and recessive. A natural

THE 'LEATHER DRESSING ROOM' at Sudeley Castle. The tones of paint are subtly adjusted to the antique leather walls and the bed's hangings.

196

Berber wool carpet, rustic but light in tone, has been used on the floor. It is, however, the blue counterpoint which is the real triumph of this scheme. The cool still blue, like an oasis in the desert, is found in the print of the old silk hangings on the four-poster bed, as well as on the tester frame and the wool bullion fringe. It is repeated in the gathered valance above the bay window and on the wing chair covered in the Colefax 'Strawberry Leaf' print. It is a colour that gives emphasis to the richness of the burnished gold and credence to the idea that this little castle bedroom has remained untouched for 250 years.

A FINE EARLY GEORGIAN ROOM. While the formal composition of furniture is appropriate for this period, the decoration is handled with greater freedom. The original panelling is painted in tones of blue in the French manner and the lively 'Charlotte' chintz is used on the bed and curtain drapes.

Chicheley Hall in Buckinghamshire was built around 1720 by Francis Smith of Warwick for Sir John Chester, a sufficiently perceptive man to have subscribed to William Kent's Grand Tour of Italy. This bedroom, with its original panelling, would have been plain and rather sparse in its early years. One imagines white painted walls, a rather severe four-poster bed dressed in damask with window curtains to match, a pair of chairs, a tallboy and a small table arranged against the walls, with a rug on a dry scrubbed floor perhaps removed in summer.

To be historically correct the redecoration might have proceeded along these lines, but Tom Parr was inclined to be more resourceful. His aim was to achieve something lighter and more expansive in effect. He took his inspiration from a bed found elsewhere in the house and as a result a more fanciful and eclectic scheme emerged. The mid eighteenth-century bed is the focus of attention and is crowned by a glorious rococo tester; the mirror above the chimney-piece echoes the highly worked form of the bed's gilded profile. Although there are pieces of furniture, like the walnut side chairs and the chest between them, which conform to the date of the house, the bed, mirror and beautiful little English painted side chair in the French taste do not. The room is a mixture and, particularly when comfortable armchairs and a skirted book table are added, it becomes a bedroom of our own time, but one that embodies the spirit of the past.

Parr has used a fabric with a complicated nineteenth-century design for the bed, curtains and upholstery. The blue colourway of the 'Charlotte' chintz is a perfect foil for the strength of the panelling, while acknowledging the presence of all the blue and white china in the room. The curtains have been finished with double pinked and scalloped frills in sympathy with the jagged form of the tester frame. The carpet is neutral in colour, but the addition of a small medallion pattern relieves the blandness. The octagonal book table provides a delightful splash of colour. The quilted cover perfectly combines with the scheme and the red of the undercloth, and happily neutralizes the riotous colours of all the jacketed books piled on top. The walls have been painted blue, not in the English manner, but in the French. The stiles and rails are the darkest blue, the panels a medium tone, with the fields to the panels a shade deeper. The mouldings are picked out in the palest off-white so that the whole wall becomes a delightful visual essay of its component parts. Pots and their supporting brackets, pictures and prints have been composed within the panels so that all has a harmony that is totally satisfying.

IN THIS SAME BEDROOM ONE can see how authoritatively the wall decoration has been built up on individual panels.

A SPLENDID EIGHTEENTH-century bed with the prettiest pierced and painted tester. The window and bed draperies use the same silk taffeta, with double scalloped, pinked and gathered frills on the bottom which unify the room.

OVERLEAF: THE DUCHESS OF Beaufort's bedroom, Badminton. The cool blue-greys of the panelling's tonal painting provide the perfect background for the 'Hops' chintz. The Duchess's bathroom beyond.

Here, in this London house, is a bed of great height and suggestive presence, a shrine to Aphrodite. Even the serpentine form of its pierced and decorated tester frame hints at sensuality. Imogen Taylor's decoration of the room is glorious; it balances richness of pattern and detail with a tranquillity of blues and white. The 'Roses and Ribbons' carpet, coloured in an abstract way with dark blue leaves on a pale blue ground interwoven with the silvery ribbons and roses, has been laid with a plain surround to give the appearance of a large rug. The ribbon design is repeated in the wallpaper, which has tiny flowers specially printed to Colefax colours by Mauny. Imogen has carried the blues up into the cornice to give an illusion of greater height.

As the bed and the bay window are equally dominant, for visual unity they have been treated in a similar fashion. All the drapes are finished in double pinked and scalloped frills in blue and white striped and off-white taffeta. There is an abundance of rhythm and detail in all this work, with its profusion of swags, *choux*, goblets and tails, giving harmony to both the bed and the window.

A nineteenth-century *chaise longue* has been covered in another

199

ribbon design chintz. It is deeply buttoned in a decidedly Victorian manner to look as if it has always been around, old, comfortable and friendly. Other pieces of furniture like the *bureau plat* and the Regency elbow chairs are light in stance and emphasize the room's femininity, while the geometry of the red quilt on the bed makes a bolder statement. It is these contrasts and anomalies that make this room such a delight.

Vivien Greenock redecorated a number of bedrooms at Badminton which are remarkable for a sense of completion that goes way beyond the norm. This is more than having appropriately chosen furniture in the right place and good pictures on the walls; it is a feeling that these rooms are an expression of the Beauforts' very individual way of life. The nuances have been understood and a balance struck between their possessions, which are a record of the family history, and the colours, fabrics and designs that visually bind everything together.

One feels the presence of the Duchess's personality in her bedroom. There is a games table with a half-completed game of patience set upon it, a favourite, rather lumpy *chaise longue*, slip-covered in blue, at the end of the bed and a big armchair with rugs thrown over it for her dog. There is also her personal choice of pictures: the group of mid nineteenth-century family portraits reminiscent of the style of Winterhalter gloriously grouped around the bed's commanding form. The colour scheme, which is similar to the bedroom at Chicheley, has panelled walls painted in blues and off-white and uses a mouseback-coloured medallion carpet. This warmish neutral tone compensates for the blues of the panelling and the cooler blue-green hues of the chintz, so that the temperature of the overall colour scheme is kept even. The curtains to the windows and drapes to the Hepplewhite

201

bed have been made in the blue colourway of the Colefax 'Hops', but are treated differently. The bed's straight pelmet is pinked and scalloped with an underfrill in blue, whereas the curtains have a serpentine-shaped valance with goblets within the gathers, a two-tone cotton rope and a block cotton fringe as enrichment. Between the curtains is a delightful compositon in *voile* – a skirted dressing table, pretty lampshades and a swagged and bowed mirror frame – all treated with the same lightness of touch. A room of this stature often benefits from the overt femininity of such details.

The principal spare room is a spectacular celebration of the chintz 'Rosa Mundi', which is used on the bed and to upholster the walls. The 'Tatton Park' carpet is composed of small green quatrefoils on a stone-coloured ground. Plain green curtains with a gathered and fringed valance hang from carved white painted pelmets matching the design of the bed. The deep pink of the Victorian buttoned sofa pays tribute to the roses in the chintz and complements this verdant theme.

The previous Duchess chose as her own bedroom the fine architectural room shown on page 184. The arrangement of columns, creating a bed alcove, harks back to the time when bedchambers were considered and used as important reception rooms. What had been Sir Robert Walpole's own chamber at Houghton, in Norfolk, has just such an alcove, as does the principal bedchamber in Roger Morris's exquisite Palladian gem, Marble Hill House, in Richmond. Whereas those bedrooms were conceived as an expression of status and authority, this room is light and charming. The panelling is painted in

THE COLOURBOARD FOR THE Duchess of Beaufort's bedroom (shown on the previous page).

THE PRINCIPAL SPARE ROOM AT Badminton and its colourboard, centred around the spectacular 'Rosa Mundi' chintz.

A CORNER OF THE PREVIOUS Duchess of Beaufort's bedroom showing the jib door into its adjacent bathroom.

BELOW: THE DUKE OF Beaufort's bedroom is an unreservedly masculine room inspired by a painting by Delacroix of the Duke of Mornay. There are very few rooms that have sufficient presence to be able to take a stripe of this scale on the walls, let alone a bedroom.

BELOW RIGHT: THE decoration of the Duke's bathroom is equally strong, with its jockey scales and painted rural screen.

three tones of off-white, in the French manner. This accent is further underlined by the Louis XVI-style bed and the delicate English chairs, also in the French taste, are painted white. The *Polanaise* tester is Continental in design, its corona suspended from cords tied with a bow. The 'Lichfield' chintz is the only patterned fabric in the room and has been confined to the bed and the smaller chairs. A pretty Georgian settee is slip-covered in the Colefax & Fowler white 'Chevron Stripe' cotton, piped in a melon colour which relates to the fabric of the French-headed curtains. The design of the curtains has been kept simple so that the rhythm of the architecture remains unchallenged.

The Duke's bedroom and bathroom are huge, unreservedly masculine, rooms. Their decoration was inspired by Delacroix's painting of the Duke of Mornay's bedroom, which is what the Duke decided he wanted for himself. As a consequence, the huge stripe, corresponding to that in the painting, was specially woven and has been applied to the walls and used as a slip-cover on the Chesterfield sofa. His Directoire bed and other upholstery are finished in a hot tomato-coloured linen and sit upon the most vigorous of English Turkey-work carpets. Colours and patterns like these would be almost impossible to use in more conventional rooms with contents of less weighty impact. The tough bracketed cornice, the monumental Kentian picture frames, the stool and the desk piled high with photographs enable this boldest of statements to triumph.

The key to the decoration of these bedrooms is 'suitability', to use Elsie de Wolfe's phrase. Fantasy and individual requirement will take many forms, but for the results to carry any authority they must be appropriate to the architectural context. So many of the buildings in which we work are traditional and these rooms reflect this fact. Antique furniture, old drawings and bits of china may be used, but this does not turn them into historical recreations. They are comfortable, practical rooms that contain the personal things that have most meaning for their owners.

CHAPTER 13   Contemporary Design

OPPOSITE: THIS LIVING ROOM has all the openness associated with modern architecture. Screens and a cylindrical steel staircase replace walls and doors in dividing up the space.

THE DESIGN OF AIRCRAFT AND boats has to be treated with greater simplicity than that of conventional interiors. In this modern boat panelled walls break up large areas of wall space and add visual interest to these surfaces.

ENTERTAINING AT HOME HAS NOW BECOME A CENTRAL FEATURE OF urban life and with this has developed pride of place – a great stimulus to interior decoration.

When designing homes in any city it is essential to understand the life that people lead; every decision has to be judged within this context. The range of interests, the manner of entertaining and the people themselves are both diverse and particular and this has to be reflected in the conception of the smallest apartment or the grandest house. The type of architecture will also have a bearing. Cities have seen such a huge range of development this century that we are faced with such anomalies as converting Regency town-house rooms into modern apartments and tempering the excesses of modern architects high on the skyline.

It is sometimes felt that the more typical Colefax & Fowler approach is too traditional or romantic in this context. Even those who would choose it for the country and for town houses sufficiently distinguished or atmospheric to invite it prefer a more pragmatic approach in certain circumstances. When it comes to high-rise living or architecture that does not lend itself to a traditional form of interpretation, the decoration must be adjusted to suit.

THE DINING ROOM AND THE view into it from the corridor.

A typical example is an apartment on the top floor of an Edwardian block in London's Mayfair. Most of the existing rooms were very small, tucked under the eaves of a mansard roof and not of a proportion appreciated by the owner; any form of design incorporating traditional details, other than certain ones already there, was rejected straightaway. The client is a bachelor who pursues a transglobal life, his enthusiasm for which has shaped the way these interiors have been conceived.

Throughout the ages Europeans have travelled and collected voraciously and their homes have usually become an expression of this worldliness. This apartment is a contemporary equivalent which has turned into a sort of metaphor for this client's life. Japanese screens, Indian and South Sea ceremonial axes are displayed cheek by jowl with modern European paintings, antiquities and African art. It is as diverse a collection of form, age and culture as one could find, all set within a framework strong enough to give it structure.

The three reception rooms that form the core of this apartment have been opened into each other, but the space has flexibility and surprise created by screens and a huge pivoting door. Everything has been kept dark in tone because these rooms are for evening entertaining. Seating areas take refuge, under pools of lamplight, from half-seen totemic forms and the dappled shadows cast by an old and much loved *ficus*.

This primitive mood is repeated in the patterns of the grey and white cotton slip-covers, Ikat cushions and the earthy colours of the upholstery. The staccato decoration of various tables veneered in Macassar ebony and sycamore burr have been designed by us to extend this spirit. On the walls, some painted a grey-white and others brown and waxed, hang a variety of pictures. Modern paintings, with their brighter colours and sharper forms, float free of their surroundings, while the nineteenth-century pictures are of distant views through which the imagination can wander.

ABOVE LEFT: THE ENTRANCE hall to a top floor apartment. The perforated screen filters the light and changes the character of a traditional window. This is essentially a space for evening use, where mirrored screens and pivoting panels expand or contain its limits.

ABOVE: EGYPTIAN FURNITURE and a distant view of Mount Ararat seen through the eyes of George Frederick Watts.

A VIGOROUS MARBLE IN A contemporary bathroom.

Small spaces mean practical bathrooms. This one has not been conceived as a sitting room in which to linger and relax, but it is nonetheless comfortable and functional. All the main surfaces are finished in a vigorous figured marble, with mirrors that pivot and magnify, the right lights in the right place and all the equipment that could possibly be needed.

Comparable to this is a house in the centre of London designed to a similar brief given by another bachelor perpetually on the move (perhaps the destiny of bachelors). His mobility is reflected in the rather sparse quality of the room illustrated here, with its comparative freedom from possessions. The area is visually broken up by screens and a circular staircase. Behind the abstract screen, designed to tone in with the upholstery colours, there is a dining table and ten chairs. The polished aluminium of the staircase's drum interior and another perforated screen tease the eye with reflections and glimpses of barely discernible images. Behind this lattice work there are further chairs and a banquette in a sea-blue that picks up the colour of the check curtains.

FURNITURE AS ART AND ART AS decoration. An interesting group is formed by a unique lamp by Alva Aalto, a Picasso pot and a pair of Vienna Secession chairs from which to survey the charmingly *denudée* showgirl.

THE LARGE PLANT FRACTURES the purity of the apartment's simple lines by breaking up the light. Mysterious totems, Japanese screens and modern paintings arrest the eye. This is an abstract space with points of interest arranged without formality.

207

The perforated screen, a type of modern Arab *mashrabiya*, enables this small space to be part of, and yet to remain separate from, the rest of the room.

A LONG VIEW DOWN THE living room showing how the geometry of the space contributes as much to the decoration as the decoration owes to geometry.

The minimalist decoration is an ideal foil for the primitive African sculpture with its heavy patination. The huge drum table of grotesque masks looks particularly well surmounted by the ugly form of the cactus. The pair of Ming chairs that face the large red sofa are a touchstone for all that is greatest in the art of furniture design. A second black lacquer pair is a turn-of-the-century Vienna Secession exercise of similar purity.

Unlike the Mayfair apartment which is dark, enveloping and designed for evening use, this house is off-white, expansive and perfect for daytime and for weekend lunches, with its glorious formal garden on a lower level. The colours of the upholstery – orange, tans and reds and cool sea-blue – are used against off-whites and the mouse-coloured Brussels weave carpet has been chosen in the old Fowler tradition, a non-colour like faded boards.

Josephine and Uberto Quintavalle bought their 1920s Chelsea house as a base for themselves and their large family. It is an example of 'freestyle architecture' borrowing liberally from Caroline, Queen Anne and Georgian buildings. They were no more interested in the formality of fine furniture than in a typically polite Georgian house with basement kitchen, children's attic bedrooms and countless stairs in between. This is a rambling house of six double bedrooms and five reception rooms on three floors only and all the decoration and contents indicate an easy, spontaneous approach to living.

The background to much of the decoration of the house is deliberately coarse, as in the ragged paintwork of the walls and the crudely woven carpet specially made for the house in Tangiers' Grand Souk. Most of the ingredients of the scheme have been chosen for their graphic quality and colour. The magnificent Heriz carpet, the orange lacquer Thai wedding basket, the green ceramic garden stool and the Anglo-Indian ebony *bergère* exemplify the choice and support the spirit of the large Roger Hilton abstract oil above the banquette. Simple Roman shades in grey and white seersucker maintain privacy and match the simplicity of the overall decoration. The whole effect is robust in a way that can accommodate the sort of randomness which one associates with the rough and tumble of family life.

The first impression of all the examples here might be that this form of decoration does not belong to the Colefax & Fowler tradition. However, the choice of upholstery, the grouping of furniture and the balance of colours – in short, the sense of comfort – is applied to these interiors every bit as carefully as to a Cotswold farmhouse or a Georgian rectory. The analysis of patterns of behaviour and the thinking behind the scale of the elements chosen and their disposition follows exactly the same rules. So the Colefax & Fowler doctrine, though less obviously, permeates these rooms just as much as the more conventional interiors in which we are involved.

BELOW RIGHT: WITH contemporary interiors, and the absence of decorative detail in fabrics and architecture, the items chosen take on greater decorative significance. The power of a Heriz carpet or the impact of a Roger Hilton painting becomes central to the room's rhythm, so that even the cushions appear to play their part in this abstract order of things.

A CLARITY OF COLOUR AND form have determined the choice of things here.

| CHAPTER 14 | # The Influence of Colefax & Fowler |

HAMPTON'S FORMAL composition between the two windows.

OPPOSITE: A NEW YORK apartment exhibiting the Colefax & Fowler influence. The American decorator Mark Hampton has used the 'Old Rose' chintz for the walls, the curtains and the upholstery, coconut matting on the floor and a mixture of furniture styles in an informal approach that resembles our own. However, his decoration has an edited feel to it which is more ordered than the English romantic spirit would choose.

IN DECORATION, THE SUCCESSION OF IDEAS AND INFLUENCES ARE AN immensely interesting phenomenon, like the flowing of a great river. As John Fowler made his way, from modest beginnings through to his important partnership with Nancy Lancaster, he absorbed and moulded ideas into his own personal style which in turn came to influence the course of design itself. Today reputations are established as much through social facility and magazine coverage as they are by word of mouth or first-hand experience of the interiors. Fowler, with his quieter tastes, shunned all forms of promotion. It was his academic approach, his appreciation of the architecture as the fundamental truth, that carried the necessary authority to further his reputation. This sense of responsibility towards his subject was in stark contrast to the popular current idea of a decorator, bouffant-crowned and with yards of tulle over one arm, proclaiming in a spirit of almost divine inspiration, 'I see it all pistachio!'.

Fowler's serious approach to decoration was appreciated not only by his private clients, especially those with fine houses, but also by such influential figures as James Lees-Milne and Christopher Hussey, the distinguished editor of *Country Life*. Moreover, Fowler impressed the National Trust representatives with whom he worked, including Robin Feddon, Christopher Wall and St John Gore. They recognized the huge contribution he was able to make to the presentation of these great houses through his fascination with the domestic detail of life. He also saw the need to treat the decoration with as much care and attention as the structure or the contents rather before the Trust had appreciated the importance of this balance. There were many architects, among them Philip Jebb and Alan Gore, for whom working with Fowler was a revelation. He brought life and point to traditional architecture and so established respect from a profession which in this century had largely scoffed at decorators.

The spread of Colefax & Fowler's influence also came about through the Brook Street shop itself. With its atmosphere of easy charm, it became a valuable catalyst for many people in their search for inspiration. Compared with the West End antique shops and galleries staffed by aloof young men eulogizing on the perfection and provenance of their stock, Colefax & Fowler seemed like a country dealer. Filled with modest antiques, painted furniture and enchantingly pretty objects, as well as useful pieces, it was always a delight to the eye. The first floor, which housed the fabrics, chintzes, papers,

carpets and stock furniture made to order, became a place of reference for the public as well as for other decorators. When Tom Parr, who initiated the retailing of all the stock items, took the step of opening the Chintz Shop in Ebury Street and other outlets all over England as well as in Edinburgh, Paris, Brussels and through Clarence House in New York, Colefax & Fowler's influence became widely recognized. Today, through the energy of our present Chief Executive, David Green, in opening further shops in the Fulham Road and Sloane Street and his perceptive acquisition of Cowtan & Tout in New York, representation is world wide.

The dissemination of ideas has also been helped by the number of people who have worked for the firm over the years. As is still the practice today, the commissions to decorate houses were traditionally undertaken with the help of young assistants. John Fowler's autocratic and temperamental personality made him notoriously difficult to work for and the few who survived managed to do so by acting as a stabilizing influence. He came to rely on the calm efficiency of his assistants in order to cope with the immense pressure of so much detailed work. They had to be talented, but in a supportive way as he would not tolerate rivalry. Imogen Taylor and George Oakes both began their careers in this way and, having stuck it out, have in turn become central to our present-day success. When Tom Parr joined he built up his own team of assistants, and now all the decorators do the same.

A HOUSE OUTSIDE CHICAGO. Here Imogen Taylor has infused something of the spirit of late eighteenth-century Scandinavian decoration. This room is clean and light in its colonial neo-Classicism.

THIS BED WAS DESIGNED BY Imogen Taylor, painted in the Colefax studio and shipped out to Chicago.

212

THE CHICAGO DINING ROOM IS a Chinoiserie fantasy painted on paper by George Oakes in England. The painted chairs and the carpet are also of our design.

A GEORGE OAKES PAINTED screen breaks up the uniformity of the walls between the windows.

It is therefore hardly surprising that the number of those who have in some way been touched by the spirit of Colefax & Fowler since the late 1940s is colossal. Some left no doubt relieved that such a painful apprenticeship was over; others were inspired by the firm's precepts and set up various enterprises on their own. Both Jean Hornak, who was with Fowler in his earliest days at 292 and is still painting, and Graham Carr, a painter who was Fowler's assistant during the last years of his life, are considered among the best in their field. Others, such as Joyce Shears and Muriel Hourigan, struck out as decorators on their own. Nina Campbell, an established London decorator, shows something of the imprint of her short stay with John Fowler, although looking back on the episode she doubts whether she was much use to him at the time. In London and the provinces there are many small decorating businesses which base their identities on the Colefax & Fowler model and which are often staffed by at least one member who has passed through the firm. The success of the fabrics, the papers and the accessories and the adaptability of this easy country style have found such an eager reception that, in its more cautious and amateur form, it has become the look of our time. Collections of fabrics by such firms as Laura Ashley, Ramm Son & Crocker and Titley & Marr have broadened the scope of this type of decoration, but the ideas still originate from the same source.

Recently, the most fertile ground for Colefax & Fowler's ideas has proved to be the east coast of the United States, and New York in particular. In fact, the seeds of this interest were sown many years before, largely by Keith Irvine and Mario Buatta, two of New York's foremost decorators. Keith Irvine had been Fowler's assistant in the late 1950s, but had left to start on his own in America at the end of the decade. Although his apprenticeship with Fowler was demanding, he remembers the testing of his memory and other exercises with gratitude, and the experience served him well. A witty and somewhat iconoclastic decorator, he has achieved a style very much of his own. His whimsical use of nineteenth-century furniture and fabrics has a richness of pattern and warmth that envelops one like Mr Dick's hospi-

tality in *David Copperfield*. His deliberate mixing of furniture styles and the jumble of bits and pieces of china, prints and needlework evoke something of Fowler before any editing has taken place. His wide use of chintz has helped to prepare the American taste for it.

Mario Buatta, who worked briefly as Irvine's assistant, met Fowler on one of his trips to England and thereafter became a firm friend and regular Christmas visitor to the Hunting Lodge. As a decorator, he unabashedly fell under Fowler's spell and proceeded to carry out a number of interiors in America that are a brighter, less 'handed down' version of his mentor's style. The appeal of his work, again dependent on an extensive use of chintzes, often Colefax & Fowler's, has furthered the general awareness of our own style. His use of fabrics and upholstery, with the balance of colours and decorative antiques, is similar to our own.

A VERY PRETTY BEDROOM decorated by Keith Irvine for his daughter. The layering of pattern and detail, to which many found and treasured possessions are then added, is typical of his work. This romantic approach is finally more concerned with the overall mood than with any individual item in the decoration.

THIS SPECTACULAR BEDROOM, designed by Mario Buatta, has much in common with the rooms in which we use draped beds. However, the serpentine form of these curtains and the degree of drama in this bedroom are more exaggerated than our own approach would allow.

'Sister' Parish, the doyen of American decoration, produces work that is as classic as it is comfortable and carries the stamp of great experience. Although she began doing up houses before Fowler, their careers largely ran parallel. At one point Nancy Lancaster proposed, due to the sympathy between their styles, a professional tie-up, but the scheme fell foul of technical legalities and so the idea came to nothing. Out of these discussions, however, grew a friendship between Mrs Parish and John Fowler and over the years 39 Brook Street became the focal point of her annual European buying trips; she was also a frequent weekend visitor to the Hunting Lodge. According to John Cornforth in his authoritative book *The Inspiration of the Past*, she declared her indebtedness to Fowler's influence and it is plain from the

MARIO BUATTA'S OWN apartment in New York.

style of her work that they had many tastes and enthusiasms in common. Her mix of English and French furniture and the subtlety of her colours mirror his own preferences, but above all they shared an essential sense of comfort.

In an article entitled 'American Greats' in the September 1988 issue of the American *House and Garden*, in which the work of eight leading firms of decorators is discussed in detail, it is revealing that, besides the three decorators mentioned above, two others, Mark Hampton and David Easton, also exhibit the influence of the English country house tradition. Both use an eclectic mixture of furniture and possessions, suggesting acquisition by inheritance or in the Grand Tour tradition, as a means of satisfying, in Mark Hampton's observation, 'the romantic longing for the ennobling past'. This style of decoration is comfortable and immensely easy to live with; it also has the merit that

it can be adapted more easily to changing tastes. Since it can be added to with a greater degree of wit and originality than is possible in any strictly period vignette, its evolution is essentially more creative and personal.

American taste in decoration is moving towards the mid-Atlantic as it discovers the sympathetic charm of this English tradition. The look that was recreated by such American luminaries as Elsie de Wolfe and Nancy Lancaster out of the elegance of a more sensitive time than our own was a reaction to the English submission to discomfort and dour living. These days, however, good English furniture is as keenly pursued in Pimlico as it is at Parke Burnet, so perhaps the style is Anglo-American after all.

From Montego Bay to Miami, New York to Nashville and many points in between, the call on Colefax & Fowler to work in the United States is greater now than ever before. Although John Fowler was the first of us to decorate in New York, for Mrs Paul Mellon, he would never cross the Atlantic himself; schemes were worked out in England with Mrs Mellon, curtains and upholstery were made here and even the painters were sent over for a two-week instruction from Fowler in the necessary techniques.

Nowadays attitudes have changed generally and there are differences between client relationships on both sides of the Atlantic. American clients demand more, expect more and bestow greater freedom than their English counterparts. In America the priorities alter,

UPHOLSTERED CHINTZ BESIDE the occasional *fautueil* in 'gauffraged' velour confirms that the spirit of John Fowler is still at work.

216

OPPOSITE: A DRAWING ROOM/ library designed by Tom Parr for a New York client. This huge room has been cleverly divided up by screens and dwarf bookcases. The balance of rich reds and variety of patterns evoke something of a nineteenth-century urban interior; however, the crispness of finish and the sense of order are unmistakably American.

A PRESENTATION BOARD FOR AN American client showing curtain designs, fabrics and photographs of rugs keyed to a coloured-up plan.

convenience technology abounds and, as everything should have its place, storage is designed as carefully as the rooms themselves. The basic intentions may start the same way, but then we carry on right through to the provision of facecloths, flowers and schemes for parties; for Americans, final presentation is everything. Their appreciation of comfortable living is highly developed. The organization of furniture is studied with the greatest of care, so that the maximum number of conversational groups can be established in drawing rooms. These rooms are conceived as personalized *mis-en-scnes* for a gathering of friends and entertaining, with a level of 'finish' and sparkle that is much more studied than our own. In this respect they are more Parisian in feel. The English preference is for a level of comfort suggested by long-established ownership, as in the wearing of a favourite tweed suit and Lobb shoes that are well into their second decade.

Whereas it is not unusual for an American client to flirt with the idea of the timeworn elegance of a well-used English interior, in the end a more polished look usually emerges. It is a matter partly of temperament, and partly of the quality of light. English light is soft, mellow and nostalgic. In spite of wide variations across the country, American light tends to be brighter and clearer than ours. This inevitably affects the colours and the thinking behind our proposals. In Chicago the light is clean, like that of Scotland; in the southern states and on the west coast it is warmer and a French palette of colours looks better.

217

The differences are, however, of emphasis rather than principle and it is evident that the English romantic look has timeless appeal. Having been the last country in Europe to come under the influence of the great Classical maturation of Italy, England seems to have held on to many aspects of the medieval passion for stylized naturalism in decoration. The preoccupation with nature and floral decoration represents a recurring theme that stretches right back in history. It can be traced from crewel work and embroidery during the reigns of the Stuarts through the profusion of needlework in the eighteenth century and comes to a head in the riot of floral decoration that was applied to almost everything in sight during the first half of the nineteenth century. This love of nature established such a firm hold on our imaginations that the tradition has never been lost. Its spirit threads its way through Colefax & Fowler's decoration in particular. While architects by and large have absolved themselves from any responsibility for humanitarian architecture, we represent one of the very few sources by which it can be achieved. It is our belief that we have become a vehicle for a tradition that will always be assured of a future because it is inextricably linked to the world of nature and the heritage of our past.

39 BROOK STREET. THROUGH the years this Colefax & Fowler showroom has represented all that we believe in – the mixture of pattern and print, useful pieces of furniture and a delight in the more modest things of life.

218

GLOSSARY

BERGÈRE	– a French wooden framed armchair with curved back and high sides, most commonly from Louis XVI period. Also gave its name to a type of English chair of similar form, but often caned instead of upholstered.
BLOCK FRINGE	– a fringe trimming coloured with equal blocks of contrasting colour.
BOUCLÉ	– a coarse woollen cloth with an uneven thickness and a knobbled surface effect.
BRUSSELS WEAVE	– a form of carpet made first in Kidderminster at the end of the eighteenth century. Woven in long narrow loom strips with a loop pile, the carpet is sewn together to fit the room and often completed with a decorative border. Brussels weave carpeting introduced the concept of the fitted carpet to English houses in the Regency period.
BULLION FRINGE	– a fringe trimming formed of twisted loops of rope. Made in either wool or silk in a variety of lengths or thicknesses.
BUREAU PLAT	– a large French writing table. The most important varieties are ornamented with boulle work.
CARTOUCHE	– a curling scroll or shield designed to hold armorial bearings.
CHOU	– from the French for 'cabbage' – an ornamental curtain detail consisting of a circular gathered piece of fabric designed to give the illusion of a curtain having been caught up.
COCKPEN CHAIR	– a type of eighteenth-century chair made from chinoiserie fretwork.
COROMANDEL	– a type of decorative veneer introduced around 1790. Stripy black to ginger yellow in colour, it is often confused with Zebra wood.
CONSOLE TABLE	– a side table supported on two bracket supports, or by an eagle.
DAMASK	– cloth, either of velvet, silk or cotton, woven or printed with a large-scale stylised floral pattern which first appeared in the seventeenth century. Also used on wallpaper where it is either printed or made as a flock pattern.
DEMI-LUNE	– literally 'half-moon', a descriptive term applied to semi-circular commodes.
DIAPER-TRELLIS	– trellis work formed of diagonal members.
DIRECTOIRE	– the severe angular style favoured by the Revolutionary bourgeoisie in the 1790s under the Directory after the Revolution in Paris.
DISTRESS	– apparent signs of wear and age in wood.
DUCHESSE	– a very large Louis XV armchair with a seat long enough to support one's legs full-stretch.
ÉTAGÈRE	– a free-standing, and often mobile, piece of furniture consisting of shelves.
EMPIRE STYLE	– style of neo-Classicism prevalent under Napoleon in France, which was richly luxurious and heavily inspired by Roman Imperial fashions.
FAUTEUIL	– a French salon armchair, with carved decoration, sometimes gilt.
FESTOON	– a curtain fixed at the top in one piece and drawn on vertical cords into swags.
FRETWORK	– pierced angular pattern used to make galleries on chinoiserie furniture, or used as 'blind' decoration when applied to solid timber.
GAUFFRAGE	– velvet with a stamped pattern.
GIMP	– woven braid used to ornament curtains, beds or chairs; can be extremely complex in form.

GIRONDOLE	– a wall sconce with a mirror placed behind for extra reflected light.
GRISAILLE	– painting in monotone usually in greys, often to imitate marble relief.
GUILLOCHE	– neo-Classical architectural ornament of interlocking circles, used as a frieze or a cornice.
TETE AUX GOBLETS	– a curtain heading where the fabric is caught into large rounded open topped pleats and held with a button.
ITALIAN STRUNG	– a way of drawing curtains where the curtains are joined at the head and the drawstrings are strung diagonally through or behind the curtain from about one third of the way down.
JAPPANNING	– the historic name for lacquer work which originates from the first appearance of this sort of furniture from Japan in the seventeenth century. See also 'Japponaise lacquer'.
LIT A LA POLONAISE	– a bed with high ends supporting an elaborately dressed dome; first appeared in the late eighteenth century.
NOILE	– a slubbed, or coarse, silk cloth.
OTTOMAN	– a ribbed, densely woven fabric of either cotton or silk.
PARQUETRY	– pattern formed by geometrical inlay.
PATERA	– classical rosette as used on ancient buildings.
CHARLES PERCIER (1764-1838)	– a French architect of great importance who worked in tandem with P.F.L. Fontaine, between 1794 and 1814, becoming the principal architects of Napoleonic Paris and progenitors of the Empire style.
PICOT BRAID	– a woven cotton braid of various widths with a bobble edging; sometimes striped.
PIER GLASS	– an ornamental looking glass hung between two windows.
PINKING	– cut with pinking shears to form a regulated jagged edge.
PINOLEUM BLIND	– a roller blind formed of thin but opaque material to diffuse light and glare.
PIPING	– fabric covered cord, used to embellish upholstery seams; frequently used with a contrasting coloured fabric.
QUATREFOIL	– four leaf-shaped curves within a circle – a motif of the Gothic style.
REGENCE	– period of the Regency of Philip of Orleans during the infancy of Louis XV. Although the Regency itself lasted 1715-23, the style lasted from 1710-30, and consisted of an early Rococo style.
RETOUR D'EGYPTE	– Egyptian Revival in France, beginning with Napoleon's conquest of Egypt in 1797.
RUCHING	– fabric gathered into regular horizontal pleats, making the effect of rows of small swags.
SCALLOPING	– a trimming formed by cutting the fabric edge with a multitude of regular semi-circles.
SECRETAIRE	– a writing desk with sloping fall front with matching stand made from 1700. Often incorporated into a drawer in the eighteenth century in a chest of drawers or in a bookcase.
SLIPPER-CHAIR	– a small upholstered side chair with curved shaped back.
STRAPWORK	– ornament of the late sixteenth century of Flemish origin comprised of scrolled and curving straps.
TOILE DE JOUY	– French printed scenic cloth made from rolled engraved copper plates. First made in 1760 at Jouy en Josas near Versailles.
TOLE	– painted tinware, popular as a medium for lamps and jardinières in the Regency period.
TORCHERA	– a tall carved candlestand.
VOILE	– a thin fine cotton fabric.
VELOURS DE LIN	– a velvet made from linen.

AUTHOR'S
ACKNOWLEDGEMENTS

This account of Colefax & Fowler's origins and the evolution of the firm's ideas has been compiled with the generous help of many people.

My thanks are due first to Elizabeth Dickson who travelled the length and breadth of Britain obtaining first-hand accounts of John Fowler's life from the many people who knew him and from others for whom he had worked. I am very grateful to Michael and Lady Anne Tree for their personal portrait of Nancy Lancaster. My indebtedness extends to many of my colleagues at Colefax & Fowler for their comments, reflections and advice, in particular to Imogen Taylor, Tom Parr, Stanley Falconer, George Oakes and Andrew Ginger. I would also like to thank Jean Hornak, Bianca and Eden Minns, Muriel Hourigan, Mrs Frank Stone, Stephen Long, Hardy Amies, Christopher Gibbs, Paul Tanqueray, Elizabeth Hanley, Barry McIntyre and the Countess of Hambledon. My thanks also go to Charlotte FitzMaurice and Caroline Dix for their assistance and especially to Sandy, my wife, for all her help, patience and very necessary common sense. I was also extremely fortunate in having a wonderful editor, Sarah Riddell, whose humour, help and advice were invaluable. Finally, I would like to express my admiration for Peter Windett who managed to create a book of such style and coherence.

PICTURE
ACKNOWLEDGEMENTS

The photographs on the following pages were specially taken for this book, and the publishers and Colefax & Fowler are most grateful to the individual owners for granting permission to include them.
Michael Laye 85, 122, 124, 126L, 127L, 130L, 170, 205L,R.
James Mortimer 48-9, 50, 51, 68, 71T, 72, 73, 77, 80T, 81, 82T,B, 84R, 88T, 89, 95L, 101T, 102B, 103, 110, 111TL,B, 112BL, 113, 115T,BL, 118BR, 120, 121, 123R, 125R, 132, 136, 145, 146, 147R, 148-155, 158, 159, 163, 164, 169, 172, 173, 175, 177, 178, 179R, 180, 181, 184, 185, 186, 187, 188-9, 194R, 195, 196, 200, 201, 202L, 203T,BL,BR.
Karen Radkai 212-3.
John Vere Brown 2, 52, 53, 54, 70B, 74B, 75B, 79, 83T, 88BL, 93, 94, 98B, 105T, 111R, 116B, 117, 119, 126R, 140L,R, 141T, 161, 165, 197, 198.

The publishers would like to thank the following for permission to use their photographs:
Arcaid/Lucinda Lambton 92.
Tim Beddow 6, 19, 23, 24, 38, 44, 45, 47, 69, 78, 83, 112TR, 115BR.
Mario Buatta 215T.B.
Colefax & Fowler 10, 80B, 82C, 96, 98T, 99L, 100B, 105BL, 114, 129, 130TR,BR, 140B, 141B, 202T,B.
Colefax & Fowler Archives 99R, 123L, 128R, 183, 217, 218.
Colefax & Fowler/Stanley Falconer 12R, 37R.
Colefax & Fowler/Chester Jones 75T, 134, 137, 138all, 139.
Colefax & Fowler/George Oakes 1, 3, 4, 25, 87, 88BR, 90-91, 107.
Colefax & Fowler/Tom Parr 102T, 147TL.
Conde Nast Publications Inc, London/House & Garden 8, 14L, 20, 21, 36, 37L.
Conde Nast Publications Inc, London/Vogue/David Montgomery 206TL,TR,B, 207R, 209L,R.
Conde Nast Publications Inc, London/Vogue/Snowdon 66, 128L.
Conde Nast Publications Inc, New York/House & Garden/Horst 74T, 125L, 179L.
Conde Nast Publications Inc. New York/House & Garden/Oberto Gili 216T,B.
Country Life 46.
Mark Hampton Inc/L. Himmel 210-11.
Jean Hornak 11, 12B, 18.
Horst 26, 28, 29BR, 30, 31, 32, 33, 34, 35, 60, 61T,B, 62, 63, 64TL,TR, 65BL,BR, 109B.
House Beautiful/David Montgomery 108, 109T, 162, 171, 174, 176, 194L.
Keith Irvine 214.
Millar & Harris 15, 17, 22.
Bianca Minns 16.
Derry Moore 39T, 40-41, 41, 42, 43, 55, 56, 61R, 65T, 71B, 97, 104, 127R.
Eric Morin 182, 192, 193L,R.
National Portrait Gallery/Paul Tanqueray 9, 25.
National Trust/Erik Pelham 58.
National Trust/Jeremy Whitaker 57.
Clay Perry 59.
Sotheby's, London 22TR /Cecil Beaton Archive 27, 29BL.
Trustees of the Victoria & Albert Museum 13, 14R, 116T.
Fritz von der Schulenburg 86B, 106.
Rupert Watts 204, 207L, 208.
Jeremy Whitaker 57T.
World of Interiors/Clive Frost 84L.
World of Interiors/James Mortimer 39B, 70T, 76T,B, 80C, 86TR,L, 95R, 118BL, 142, 144, 190, 191L,R.
World of Interiors/Fritz von der Schulenburg 77B, 166, 168.
World of Interiors/Christopher Simon Sykes 100T, 156.

INDEX